Concept-Based
Curriculum
AND
Instruction

In loving memory of my father, Elmer F. Keturi,
an Alaskan pioneer with a cache of great stories.

Concept-Based
Curriculum
AND
Instruction

Teaching
Beyond the Facts

H. Lynn Erickson

Foreword by Carol Ann Tomlinson

CORWIN PRESS, INC.
A Sage Publications Company
Thousand Oaks, California

For information:

Corwin Press, Inc.
A Sage Publications Company
2455 Teller Road
Thousand Oaks, California 91320
E-mail: order@corwinpress.com

SAGE Publications Ltd.
6 Bonhill Street
London EC2A 4PU
United Kingdom

SAGE Publications India Pvt. Ltd.
M-32 Market
Greater Kailash I
New Delhi 110 048 India

Printed in the United States of America

Library of Congress Cataloging-in-Publication Data

Erickson, H. Lynn.
Concept-based curriculum and instruction: Teaching beyond the facts /
H. Lynn Erickson; foreword by Carol Ann Tomlinson.
    p. cm.
Includes bibliographical references and index.
ISBN 0-7619-4639-X — ISBN 0-7619-4640-3 (pbk.)
    1. Curriculum planning—United States. 2. Education—Curricula—
Standards—United States. 3. Inter disciplinary approach in education—
United States. I. Title.
LB2806.15 .E75 2002
374'.001—dc21   2002002771

This book is printed on acid-free paper.

02   03   04   05   06   10   9   8   7   6   5   4   3   2   1

Production Editor: Diane S. Foster
Typesetter: Tina Hill
Cover Designer: Tracy Miller

Contents

Foreword

In a captivating story about a young girl at the turn of the 20th century, Dorothy Canfield Fisher (1917/1999) sees learning through the eyes of a child. The main character in *Understood Betsy* has, in all her three school years, been a "good" student. That is, she learned what she was told and gave it back accurately when questioned. In a magical moment in her third-grade year, Betsy has an encounter with another kind of learning.

On her first day at an aunt's house in the country, Betsy wakes, disoriented and apprehensive about her unfamiliar surroundings. Her aunt wisely understands the need to help the little girl "own" what happens around her, so she asks Betsy to help with churning the day's supply of butter. As Betsy turns the paddle in the big churn, her aunt talks about the women who have turned the paddle before her—a parade of women who represent both change and stability in the world. As her aunt talks, she helps Betsy measure out ingredients with precision. "She weighed out the salt needed on the scales, and was very much surprised to see that there is such a thing as an ounce. She had never met it before outside the pages of her history book and she didn't know it lived anywhere else" (pp. 57-58). The work is laced with the aunt's stories about the churn. Once again, Betsy is caught short.

> Now for a moment, she stood staring up at Aunt Abigail's face, and yet not seeing her at all because she was thinking so hard.... Why, there were real people living when the Declaration of Independence was signed—real people, not just history people.... To tell the honest truth, although she had passed a very good

examination in the little book on American history they had studied in school, Betsy had never to that moment had any notion that there ever had been really and truly any Declaration of Independence at all. It had been like the ounce, living only inside her schoolbooks for little girls to be examined about. And now Aunt Abigail, talking about a butter pat, had brought it to life. (pp. 59-60)

Educators have known for more than a hundred years what Aunt Abigail knew a hundred years ago. Facts devoid of meaning are stillborn. When we deliver information to students without breathing life into it, we have done no more than throw sand in their faces.

Now, close to a century later, Phil Schlechty (1997) reminds us again. "Students are not products. They are people with motives, wills, capacities, needs to be satisfied, desires, longings. They are not clay to be molded or widgets on an assembly line, though sometimes they must feel as though they are" (p. 58). He calls us again to the one immutable job of schools: "The business of schools is to produce work that engages students, that is so compelling that students persist when they experience difficulties, and that is so challenging that students have a sense of accomplishment, of satisfaction—indeed, of delight, when they successfully accomplish the tasks assigned" (p. 58). The job of the teacher is, as it has always been, to make learning so compelling that young people find it more satisfying to learn than to attend to any one of a score of competing possibilities.

So what does it mean to develop curriculum that compels the young mind? Once again, we know the answers to that question. They are not new, although our depth of knowledge about them is richer and fuller than in the past. Among the characteristics of such curriculum are the following:

- It is attached to the lives and cultures of learners and to the world beyond the classroom door.
- It attracts students.
- It is based on the principles of knowledge that support experts in problem solving and knowledge production in a discipline.

- It consistently fuels in-depth student understanding by guiding students in making sense of their worlds.

- It helps students organize and retain the important ideas and skills in a discipline; it provides coherence to bodies of knowledge.

- It moves beyond information to thought and to thinking about one's own thought processes.

- It actively involves students as doers and problem solvers.

- It calls on students to use what they learn in ways that demonstrate the efficacy of the ideas and skills.

- It is designed to support transfer of learning.

- It results in students' learning those things recognized by experts in a discipline, adult members of the community, and the society as having enduring value (see, e.g., National Research Council, 1999; Schlechty, 1997).

What does Lynn Erickson's work have to do with Betsy and our best knowledge of education? This book is the best tool I know to help us as teachers learn to move from knowledge on the shelf to the stuff that commends learning as a lifelong satisfaction. Lynn Erickson shows us how to live at once in both standards-based classrooms and meaning-driven classrooms. She helps us understand the roles and relationships of all elements of curriculum: facts, concepts, principles, skills, and attitudes. Her work guides us, as the title suggests, in using, but moving beyond the facts.

It is my experience that many teachers want to do with their subjects what Aunt Abigail knew to do. Many understand the truth in Phil Schlechty's challenge. Many aspire to measure their work according to a list of characteristics of best-practice curriculum. Most of us, however, have simply no idea how to move ourselves systematically from knowledge that lives in books to knowledge that lives in students.

Lynn Erickson understands the journey we need to take. She has mapped it out in this book in a way that doesn't minimize the complexity of the change but that supports us in complex change. She pays us the compliment of believing we can think in more complex, abstract, and meaningful ways about what we teach.

For me, the book is a desirable blend of theory, practice, and illustration. Its explanations are clear, and the translation of those explanations into classroom examples helps me move from vision to implementation. The book has clarified for me what it means to think about a discipline in the way an expert would—what it means to help students construct frameworks of meaning in a discipline, what it means to develop both curriculum and assessments that are catalysts for relevance, coherence, connectivity, and power.

I am a better teacher for the time I have spent studying the first edition of *Concept-Based Curriculum and Instruction*. My students are better educators and educational leaders for the time we have spent visiting and revisiting the book together. I find that each time I reread it, I become a little more like Aunt Abigail. It makes me want to keep teaching and learning for a long time.

—CAROL ANN TOMLINSON
PROFESSOR OF EDUCATIONAL
LEADERSHIP, FOUNDATIONS, & POLICY
CURRY SCHOOL OF EDUCATION
UNIVERSITY OF VIRGINIA

References

Fisher, D. (1999). *Understood Betsy.* New York: Henry Holt. (Original work published 1917)

National Research Council. (1999). *How people learn: Brain, mind, experience, and school.* Washington, DC: National Academy Press.

Schlechty, P. (1997). *Inventing better schools: An action plan for educational reform.* San Francisco: Jossey-Bass.

Preface

In school districts across the United States, the tension to meet academic standards is high because the stakes are high. General views of education are fueled by the publication of school test scores in local newspapers. The legislative push for school vouchers and the creation of a plethora of private school models—from home-schooling to for-profit, business-run schools—chips away at the traditional public school model. National and state standards are developed to bring structure to the curriculum of what students should know and be able to do.

Concept-Based Curriculum and Instruction: Teaching Beyond the Facts takes a step back and considers the conventional model of curriculum design in the United States related to the issue of standards. Does "raising standards" mean learning more content, which is delineated through "objectives"? Or does it mean using critical content as a tool to understanding key concepts and principles of a discipline, and applying understanding in the context of a complex performance? From a review of national standards, it is clear that most disciplines favor the latter goal. Certainly, knowing (and often memorizing) a body of critical content knowledge is important for an educated person. But conventional models of curriculum design have focused so heavily on the information level that most teachers lack training for teaching beyond the facts. Yet the standards and newer assessments assume that students will demonstrate complex thinking, deeper understanding, and sophisticated performance.

This book extends the ideas I presented in *Stirring the Head, Heart and Soul: Redefining Curriculum and Instruction* (Corwin Press, 1995; second edition, 2002), and it discusses the essential nature of the concept-based curriculum and instruction for the standards movement. In Chapter 1, sampling of the national content standards is reviewed through a set of concept-based questions in order to understand the differences between concept-based and topic-based design models.

The thread throughout this book is the power of a concept-based model for

- Taking thinking beyond the facts to facilitate deep understanding and the transfer of knowledge
- Systematically developing a conceptual schema in the brain to handle new information
- Meeting higher academic standards related to content knowledge, process abilities, and quality performance

The goal of this book is to raise awareness of the differences between topical and concept-based models of curriculum and instruction, and to provide some concept-based examples from different school districts around the country. This book presents components that are critical in a quality concept-process design model, but it leaves the formatting of documents up to the discretion of districts.

A discussion of the critical components for a concept-process curriculum are presented in Chapter 2 in the context of a systems design. The need for balance between process and content expectations and the requirements for each strand lead into the chapters on the integrated curriculum and instruction.

Chapter 3 presents a detailed plan for designing concept-process integrated units. Examples from school districts illustrate the role of concepts in taking thinking beyond the facts and maintaining the integrity of different disciplines in the integration process. Unit planning pages show the integral relationship between critical content, essential enduring understandings (conceptual ideas), essential questions, and student activities. The unit as a whole is coherent and focused. Instruction flows from the unit plan to engage students with higher-level thinking and understanding.

This book deals with assessment only as it pertains to the design of performance tasks and scoring guidelines for instructional units. Many books focused on assessment are currently being published that can be used to supplement the information provided in this book. Some suggestions are *Educative Assessment: Designing Assessments to Inform and Improve Student Performance* by Grant Wiggins, 1998, Jossey-Bass; *Student-Centered Classroom Assessment* by Richard J. Stiggins, 1997, Prentice Hall; and *The High Performance Toolbox* by Spence Rogers and Shari Graham, 1997, Peak Learning Systems.

Chapter 4 considers the value of a concept-process curriculum integration model in school-to-work programs. We need a new paradigm to bridge the curriculums of academic and occupational areas. This book suggests that the bridge occurs at the level of integrating concepts, which can be understood and exemplified through the content of academic courses and the performance of occupational courses.

Finally, we hear from the teachers who break new ground in the design and implementation of idea-centered teaching and learning. Excerpts from teaching units, and observations and insights on what it means to teach conceptually, expand our understanding and raise new questions.

The intended audiences for this book include the following:

- District- and site-level administrators who are responsible for curriculum, instruction, and assessment
- Teachers in leadership positions working on standards issues related to curriculum and instruction at either the district or site level
- Teachers working in teams on the development of their own classroom units
- Staff development personnel at the local, regional, or state level
- University professors and supervisors in curriculum and instruction at the undergraduate and graduate levels of teacher training

Learning how to design a curriculum that facilitates complex thinking and deeper levels of understanding is an unfolding process. This book shares some perspectives from this point in time. Readers are invited to add their thoughts and experiences to this journey. My e-mail address is hlynn@att.net.

It is an honor to have the foreword to this book written by Carol Ann Tomlinson. Her notable work with differentiated curriculum and instruction compliments and exemplifies the principles expressed in this book. Carol Ann is an "Aunt Abigail" for educators eager to learn how to meet the needs of all students in their classrooms.

My deepest gratitude goes to Eileen McMackin, Lake Washington School District, Redmond, Washington, for reviewing this manuscript and offering many suggestions for refinement; to Sally Lorenz-Reeves, Leanna Isaacson, Dr. Rosemarie Carroll, Dr. Lois Lanning, Dr. Carol Webb, Kathy Erickson, Dr. Mabel Schumacher, and many other friends and associates who have discussed and worked through these ideas in their districts. And finally, my biggest debt of gratitude goes to the teachers all over this country who have worked so hard to design quality concept-process units to raise the level of instruction and to take teaching and thinking beyond the facts. They are my teachers, for they challenge my thinking.

About the Author

H. Lynn Erickson is an independent consultant assisting schools and districts around the country with curriculum design. From 1987 to 1994, she was Director of Curriculum for the Federal Way Public Schools in Federal Way, Washington. She is a recognized presenter at national conferences and is featured in the videos, "Creating Concept-Based Curriculum for Deep Understanding" (produced by Teachstream), and "Planning Integrated Units: A Concept-based Approach (produced by the Association for Supervision and Curriculum Development). She is the author of *Stirring the Head, Heart, and Soul: Redefining Curriculum and Instruction, Second Edition* (Corwin Press, 2001).

She was born and raised in Fairbanks, Alaska, the daughter of a pioneering gold miner and a first-grade teacher. She graduated from the University of Alaska in 1968 and taught first, second, fourth, and fifth grades, as well as combination classes, while in California. She also served as a reading specialist before moving with her family to

Missoula, Montana. At the University of Montana, she earned master's and doctorate degrees in Curriculum and Instruction and Advanced School Administration. She worked as the Curriculum Coordinator for Missoula's Public Schools before becoming an elementary principal for 6 years in Libby, Montana.

She and Ken Erickson have two grown children, Kelly and Kenneth; a daughter-in-law, Jodie Erickson; a son-in-law, Patrick Cameron; and two grandsons, Trevor and Conner Cameron. They live in Washington state, and she sees them often. When she isn't traveling to school districts, she enjoys motorcycling and in-line skating with Ken.

❦ 1 ❧

Interpreting and Aligning National, State, and Local Standards

Why Standards?

When the United States had an economy that operated to a large extent within its borders and was based more on local industry and national corporations, the concern over education was not as pronounced. But the development of technology, transportation, and communication changed the face of business, and the national economy became a global enterprise. Suddenly, American business began to realize that workers needed higher levels of technological, academic, and work skills in order for industries to compete on the global stage. Parents, worried that their children would not be prepared for further schooling or work, joined with business in calling for higher educational standards.

Growing concern resulted in the launching of the 1990 National Education Goals under the Bush administration, followed by the America 2000 Act in 1991. Reform efforts continued under the administration of President Clinton with the passage of the Goals 2000 legislation in 1994. This legislation was the springboard for the development of national standards in almost every discipline of study. These documents, developed by broad-based committees of experts and professionals in each field, are invaluable to state and local districts as they design and align their own curricular frameworks. To carry out this work, however, curriculum committees need to understand how national standards are organized and the degree to which they facilitate conceptual thinking and teaching beyond the facts.

This chapter reviews a sampling of national standards from a design perspective that values concept-process curricula. This design model emphasizes the development of conceptual understanding, critical content knowledge, and performance abilities. Critical content serves as a tool for developing conceptual understanding that transfers through time. Although the review will point out design weaknesses and strengths in various national standards, it is important to realize that all of the standards have made a vital contribution to the definition of curriculum content and process.

The standards are especially important to curriculum design committees at the state and local levels for the following reasons:

- The information base has expanded so rapidly that it is difficult for curriculum committees to decide what is really "essential knowledge and skills."

- Education can be an isolated activity. It is quite easy to go into the classroom and teach from a textbook (that might well be 10 years old) and not consciously realize the depth and breadth of curricular change being demanded by a rapidly changing society.

- Designing quality curricula is a complex, intellectual task. It takes time, conceptual thinking, and design ability, as well as a thorough knowledge of a discipline. Committees made up of some of the best minds in the country developed national standards based on what students must know and be able to do in the complex, globally interdependent society of the 21st century.

- National standards provide state and local committees with a direction and focus as they undertake the critically important task of curriculum design. Key concepts and principles, critical content knowledge, and major processes and skills essential to the various disciplines are identified in the national documents.

- The national standards documents, in most cases, provide a wealth of background knowledge and information to support educators in the field as they teach essential knowledge and skills. To reconceptualize both curriculum and instruction in response to our rapidly changing society, teachers themselves need to develop deeper conceptual and content knowledge across the disciplines. The national standards are a valuable resource for teachers as they pursue a deeper understanding of their disciplines.

This chapter will review the design of a sampling of national standards through the eyes of a concept-process curriculum in order to realize the impact on classroom instruction. We will consider some review questions and then discuss the weaknesses and strengths of different standards related to higher-level conceptual thinking. We will also look briefly at a sampling of state and local standards using the same concept-based criteria and provide some design suggestions to support thinking beyond the facts. But first, we need to understand what is meant by "performance-based standards" and how this approach to assessing student work is playing out in standards documents and classroom practice.

Performance-Based Standards

Advances in brain research and knowledge of how children learn supports the notion that students must be actively engaged in learning. If knowledge is going to be retained and understood, then students must use it in a demonstration or complex performance (Caine & Caine, 1991; Perkins, 1992). This movement is a reaction against curriculum designs that list pages of objectives driven by lower-level cognitive verbs such as *list, define,* and *identify.* The lower-level recall does not require that students internalize knowledge to the point of being able to use it in complex performance.

As a result of this drive to engage students with performance, national standards committees addressed the question, "How can we circumscribe the essential content and processes of this discipline in a design format that will encourage performance?" But bringing theory and practice together through the design and writing of standards and curricula is a difficult task. Writing is thinking—and the arrangement of words on paper to effect instructional improvement in the classroom is a sophisticated task.

The committees realized that they could not write a single performance joining a process skill and a critical content topic because understanding can be demonstrated across multiple types of performances, from oral presentations to visual displays to product demonstrations. So, in most cases, committees wrote the standards as statements of content or process that students should "understand," and they followed these statements with "sample" performances; or else they fell back to traditional objectives, such as "explain" or "evaluate," which could then be demonstrated in different ways. But either way, in most cases, the resulting standards fall short of their full potential for making an impact on student learning. Are we missing a critical design component as we encourage performance to demonstrate deep understanding? I think so.

The Missing Link
in Performance-Based Theory

The idea that teachers can develop performances that demonstrate deep understanding assumes that they have consciously identified the kinds of deep understandings that the performance should demonstrate. But this skill of thinking beyond the facts has not been required in the traditional topic-based designs. Consequently, in elementary classrooms around the country, performances are more often activities (e.g., a Thanksgiving feast) related to a topic (early colonists and Indians) named in a standard. At the secondary level, instructional activities and assessments usually focus on seeking and sharing facts on the topics to be covered. Why these shallower demonstrations of understanding? Could the problem lie in the traditional curriculum design that drives instruction?

The Structure of Knowledge and
the Traditional Design of a Curriculum

Figure 1.1 displays the structure of knowledge. The traditional design of a curriculum emphasizes the lower cognitive levels, centering around topics and related facts. This curriculum design, which

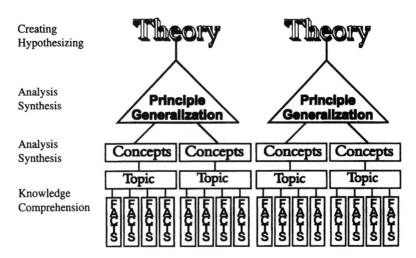

Figure 1.1. Structure of Knowledge

has been driving teaching and learning in our country for more than 100 years, must be addressed if we are ever going to raise educational standards. It does little good to engage students with performance if our curriculum design aims the display of understanding no higher than the topic.

When we address only the key concepts of disciplines offhand-edly within topics of study, we are assuming that teachers know and are drawing out the key conceptual understandings (principles and generalizations) from a topic. In fact, this is usually not happening. William H. Schmidt, research coordinator for the Third International Mathematics and Science Study (TIMSS), stated that American education covers far more content than other industrialized nations, but it lacks depth of treatment. The 1996 TIMSS study, the largest comparative international study of education ever conducted, measured the mathematics and science achievement of a half-million students at five grade levels. American students scored about average in mathematics and slightly above average in science. A follow-up study with the National Center for Improving Science Education reviewed the mathematics and science curricula for 50 countries. The researchers concluded that, comparatively, the "American science and mathematics curriculum is a mile wide and an inch deep" (Viadero, 1997, p. 6). They used the comparison that American eighth graders often lug around science textbooks of approximately 800 pages, covering more than 65 topics; yet students in Japan or Germany typically use 150- to 200-page textbooks with as few as five topics (Viadero, 1997).

How is it that other industrialized nations, such as Japan or Germany, can score better than the United States on international exams when they focus on far fewer topics? And how do they make the decisions as to which topics to include in the curriculum? The answers to these questions relate directly to the chosen emphases for curricular and instructional design.

Japan, Singapore, and other higher-scoring nations center both curriculum and instruction around the understanding of discipline-based concepts and principles (see Figure 1.1). They use topics and facts as tools to help students develop deeper understanding. This conceptual focus allows them to reduce the number of topics covered, because many topics exemplify the same concepts and conceptual understandings. Honoring elders is a Japanese tradition. These concepts of "honor" and "tradition," and the associated understandings, are characterized through a wide variety of family, civic, and ceremonial situations.

Another difference between the United States and higher-scoring nations in the TIMSS study relates to instruction. Teachers in the United States feel compelled to "cover" the abundant subject area content in the textbooks and curriculum guides. This coverage pressure reduces the amount of time available for students to problem solve and think beyond the facts. It also encourages didactic lecture formats rather than active student learning.

From 1997 news reports quoting current research, we also know that students in the United States are still entering secondary and postsecondary schools with many misconceptions related to the key concepts that frame the knowledge of a discipline. This problem is discussed clearly in David Perkins's timeless book *Smart Schools: Better Thinking and Learning for Every Child* (1992). Citing a variety of research studies, Perkins states, "One of the discomforting disclosures of the past two decades has been students' fragile grasp of many key concepts in science and mathematics. Students commonly display naive ideas about things even after considerable instruction" (p. 23).

Perkins also discusses how the packaging of information to be learned affects student retention and transfer. He relates an experiment conducted by cognitive psychologist John Bransford and colleagues:

> Some students read about nutrition, water as a standard of density, solar-powered airplanes, and other matters in the usual textbookish way, with the intent to remember. Other students read the same items of information in the context of thinking about the challenges of a journey through a South American jungle. For instance, the students read about the density of water in the context of how much water the travelers would have to carry. (Perkins, 1992, p. 22)

Perkins (1992) recounts that when both groups of students were given the task of planning a desert expedition, the students who had studied the information in the conventional way failed to transfer much of the learning into the task. But the students who had studied the information in the problem-solving context of the jungle journey made "rich and extensive use" of the information.

Certainly, providing a problem-solving context for actively engaging students in the thoughtful application of knowledge is an important variable in increasing learning. But another important variable is evident in the example. Students were required to put a "conceptual lens" on the problem-solving study. Student thinking was forced beyond the facts to the conceptual level as each topic was filtered through the bigger idea—how people meet challenges on a journey. The conceptual lens of "meeting challenges" focused the study and required students to use higher-level, integrative thought processes.

The move to require performance with knowledge is a step in the right direction. But in curriculum documents across the country, these performances will continue to fall, too often, to the level of shallow activities unless we change the focus of the curriculum and instruction from teaching topics to "using" topics to teach and assess deeper, conceptual understanding. Teachers need more training in how to think beyond the facts, to understand the conceptual structure of the disciplines, and to have the ability to clearly identify key ideas that illustrate deep knowledge. Deep knowledge transfers across time and cultures and provides a conceptual structure for thinking about related and new ideas.

Trying to teach in the 21st century without a conceptual schema for knowledge is like trying to build a house without a blueprint. Where do the pieces go? It is too late to wait until high school and college to "dump" key concepts and conceptual ideas on students. Conceptual development is a lifelong developmental process. Conceptual understanding requires a higher-level, integrative thinking ability that needs to be taught systematically through all levels of schooling. Integrated thinking is the ability to insightfully draw patterns and connections between related facts, ideas, and examples, and to synthesize information at a conceptual level. Well-designed curriculum documents can facilitate this teaching/learning process. So, how do national standards shape up in supporting the design of conceptually based curricula and instruction? (Note: The following review does not address the national English standards for the simple reason that English is not concept based—it is process and skill driven. Literature is the content and the concept-based area of the language arts.)

National Standards
Through a Concept-Process Lens

Let's apply a set of questions to review some of the national documents from a concept-process design perspective:

1. Do the standards clearly identify and highlight "integrating concepts" to facilitate integrated thinking within and across disciplines?
2. Do the standards provide a systematic and developmental conceptual schema for building deep understanding over time?
3. Is the critical content (topics of study) clearly identified by grade bands?
4. Is the critical content correlated to disciplinary concepts and conceptual ideas (essential understandings, generalizations, principles)?
5. Are processes (complex performances) and key skills clearly identified?
6. Do the processes and skills reflect the professional performances and skills of the discipline?

7. Are processes and key skills clearly differentiated from content understandings?

8. Do the standards suggest performances that demonstrate conceptual understanding?

9. Do the standards provide background information for the teacher on key concepts and critical content?

Reviewing National Standards—
What Have We Here?

Science Standards

The design award, from a concept-process perspective, goes to the national science standards (National Research Council, 1996). Based on the concept-process evaluation questions, these standards are particularly impressive.

1. Do the standards clearly identify and highlight "integrating concepts" to facilitate integrated thinking within and across disciplines?

- A set of "unifying concepts" provide a conceptual lens to facilitate "integrated thinking" as students draw from the fact base and see the patterns and connections of science at a deeper level of conceptual understanding (see Chart 1.1). Students begin to understand specific topics, such as "weather," or "the human body," not simply as a set of facts to be memorized, but as representative examples of a bigger and more abstract conceptual idea—"systems." What lessons can be learned about the interdependence and importance of systems with the study of each new example from weather systems to human body systems? Students build conceptual sophistication throughout the grades, and new information finds a home.

2. Do the standards provide a systematic schema for building conceptual understanding over time?

- The national science standards systematically and purposefully build a conceptual mental schema for understanding

Concepts	Processes
Systems, order	Organization
Evidence, models	Explanation
Change, constancy	Measurement
Evolution, equilibrium	
Form, function	

Chart 1.1. Unifying (Integrating) Concepts and Processes for Science

SOURCE: Reprinted with permission from *National Science Education Standards* by the National Research Council. Copyright © 1996 by the National Academy of Sciences. Courtesy of the National Academy Press, Washington, DC.

Grades K-4	Grades 5-8	Grades 9-12
Properties of objects and materials	Properties and changes of properties in matter	Structure of atoms
Position and motion of objects	Motions and forces	Structure and properties of matter
Light, heat, electricity, and magnetism	Transfer of energy	Chemical reactions
		Motions and forces
		Conservation of energy and increase in disorder
		Interactions of energy and matter

Chart 1.2. Excerpt From National Physical Science Standards

SOURCE: Reprinted with permission from *National Science Education Standards* by the National Research Council. Copyright © 1996 by the National Academy of Sciences. Courtesy of the National Academy Press, Washington, DC.

science and our world. Concepts spiral through the grades, and the related content topics become more sophisticated (see Chart 1.2). Consequently, the conceptual understandings stated as "supporting ideas" in the document also become more sophisticated.

3-4. Is the critical content clearly identified by grade bands? Is the critical content correlated to disciplinary concepts and conceptual ideas (essential understandings, generalizations, principles)?

- The critical content of fact-based material is clearly listed by grade bands, but the topics are not the endpoint for study. They serve as a tool for understanding the "supporting ideas" that are the deeper, essential understandings of study. The supporting ideas (Chart 1.3) are generalizations that transfer. Students can use these generalizations to build greater conceptual understanding as they meet new examples. Notice how the supporting ideas grow in sophistication through the grade bands.

5-7. Are processes (complex performances) and key skills clearly identified? Do the processes and skills reflect the professional performances and skills of the discipline? Are processes and key skills clearly differentiated from content understandings?

- The focus on "inquiry" and other key processes of science allow students to be thinkers and learners. Inquiry facilitates understanding of the conceptually based supporting ideas. The processes and skills defined in the science standards reflect the work of the professional scientist and are clearly differentiated from the content standards.

8. Do the standards suggest performances that demonstrate conceptual understanding?

- The science standards suggest activities requiring inquiry and the use of process with content.

9. Do the standards provide background information for the teacher on key concepts and critical content?

- Each standard has developmentally appropriate background information to guide the teacher. The guide to the content standard states clearly the fundamental concepts, principles,

Grades K-2	Grades 5-8	Grades 9-12
An object's motion can be described by locating it relative to another object or the background.	The motion of an object can be described by its position, direction of motion, and speed. That motion can be measured and represented on a graph.	Objects change their motion only when a net force is applied. Laws of motion are used to calculate precisely the effects of forces on the motion of objects. The magnitude of the change in motion can be calculated using the relationship F=ma, which is independent of the nature of the force. Whenever one object exerts force on another, a force equal in magnitude and opposite in direction is exerted on the first object.
The position and motion of objects can be changed by pushing or pulling. The size of the change is related to the strength of the push or pull.	An object that is not being subjected to a force will continue to move at a constant speed and in a straight line.	Gravitation is a universal force that each mass exerts on any other mass. The strength of the gravitational attractive force between two masses is proportional to the masses and inversely proportional to the square of the distance between them.
Sound is produced by vibrating objects. The pitch of the sound can be varied by changing the rate of vibration.	If more than one force acts on an object along a straight line, then the forces will reinforce or cancel one another, depending on their direction and magnitude. Unbalanced forces will cause changes in the speed or direction of an object's motion.	The electric force is a universal force that exists between any two charged objects. Opposite charges attract while like charges repel. The strength of the force is proportional to the charges and, as with gravitation, inversely proportional to the square of the distance between them.
		Between any two charged particles, electric force is vastly greater than the gravitational force. Most observable forces such as those exerted by a coiled spring or friction may be traced to electric forces acting between atoms and molecules.

Chart 1.3. Excerpt From Physical Science Supporting Ideas

and generalizations that support the standard. Teachers should teach to these ideas using the specific topics as their instructional content tool.

History Standards

The national standards for history (National Center for History in the Schools, 1996) facilitate topic-based, rather than concept-based, models of curriculum and instruction. This emphasis is illustrated in Figure 1.2. Although the standards emphasize the use of a range of thinking strategies framed by the "Historical Thinking" processes, the essential "Historical Understandings" seldom take the thinking processes beyond the analysis of facts related to specific events or figures from the past. They do, however, cause students to think critically and in depth about particular events and situations of the past.

For each standard related to a particular topic of history, there is a set of content-based understandings elaborated with objectives requiring different historical thinking skills. Figure 1.3 shows a sample standard, with content understanding and elaborated objectives.

From this design, it appears that the national history standards value specific content knowledge, as well as the ability to use historical thinking abilities related to specific events or figures, above conceptual understanding and the transfer of knowledge. In fact, many historians resist the tendency to generalize knowledge because conditions of history change, and there is danger in generalizing too freely. This is a valid concern in some respects, but what are we sacrificing by focusing historical thinking almost solely on past events? Won't students gain greater insight into the deeper lessons of history if they learn to apply historical thinking beyond the specific events to conceptual and transferable understandings?

If we choose to view "essential understandings" as the most important facts and process skills to encompass a discipline, then perhaps we would vote for the national history standards. They thoroughly define the fact base to be covered, and the portrayal of historical thinking skills is very helpful. But the heavy sail of content understandings fails to address two key points.

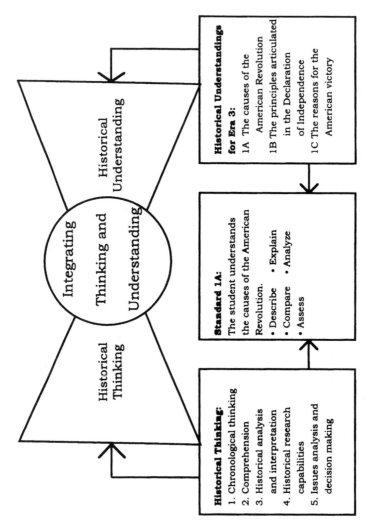

Figure 1.2. Integrating Historical Thinking and Historical Understanding, National History Standards
SOURCE: Reprinted by permission of the National Center for History in the Schools. Copyright © 1996.

Standard 1:   The causes of the American Revolution, the ideas and interests involved in forging the revolutionary movement, and the reasons for the American victory.

1A: The student understands the causes of the American Revolution.

Grades 5-12   Explain the consequences of the Seven Years' War and the overhaul of English imperial policy following the Treaty of Paris in 1763. *(Marshal evidence of antecedent circumstances.)*

Grades 7-12   Analyze political, ideological, religious, and economic origins of the revolution. *(Analyze multiple causation.)*

Grades 9-12   Reconstruct the arguments among patriots and loyalists about independence and draw conclusions about how the decision to declare independence was reached. *(Consider multiple perspectives.)*

Figure 1.3. Elements of a History Standard

SOURCE: Reprinted by permission of the National Center for History in the Schools. Copyright © 1996.

- There is no provision in the national history standards for handling the massive amount of historical information on the horizon. Are we to just keep adding addendums of complex historical information to be analyzed and memorized? And even if we add a history course every year, how can we cover so much material and still engage students' minds with the deeper lessons of history? Why must we wait for historians to provide analyses of the past before we can apply "historical thinking"? Shouldn't students be encouraged to apply the skills of historical thinking to contemporary as well as past history and, as citizens, learn how to critically construct personal meaning from multiple perspectives?

- The national history standards lack a clear conceptual structure. The focus on the fact base, without a conceptual lens to draw thinking to the integration and transfer level, leaves us traipsing over trivia in a frenetic race to cover more, faster. Figure 1.2 shows thinking and understanding becoming integrated when historical thinking processes are applied to content; but this is not conceptually integrated thinking because the patterns and connections apply only to a particular topic of study. The transferable lessons of history occur when students have learned how to see patterns and connections through time and across cultures. This meta-analytic ability needs to be developed over time by considering specific topics and facts in the broader context.

Perhaps academic historians believe that teachers will automatically draw the lessons of history out of fact-based study. But this is a dangerous assumption. Or, perhaps many historians equate fund of information with deep knowledge.

Social Studies Standards

The National Standards for the Social Studies (National Council of Social Studies [NCSS], 1994) provide a nice balance to the national history standards. I recommend that curriculum committees use both documents in developing district frameworks and school curricula. The history standards provide more than enough critical content to fill 13 years, and the social studies standards provide a conceptual structure and the beginning of an idea-centered curriculum to frame the content. The NCSS standards state that they did not intend to define the precise content of the social studies but would leave that task to the specific disciplines in the field. Therefore, committees can look to the history, geography, economics, and civics and government standards for the detail of content.

It is the conceptual structure and integrative factors that make the NCSS standards document so valuable to curriculum developers. Ten conceptual themes in the social studies standards organize the essential understandings at early grades, middle grades, and high school. Each of the conceptual themes represents a primary discipline emphasis in the social studies. This is a powerful design scheme, for it values the integrity of each discipline in the social studies. Figure 1.4 names the 10 conceptual themes and shares the major discipline emphases.

National Council for the Social Studies
Ten Conceptual Themes

Culture..Integrated Social Studies

Time, Continuity, and Change.. History

People, Places, and Environments.. Geography

Individual Development and Identity.............Psychology; Anthropology

Individuals, Groups, and Institutions.............. Sociology; Anthropology;
Psychology; Political Science; History

Power, Authority, and Governance.........................Government; Politics;
Political Science; History; Law;
other social sciences

Production, Distribution, and Consumption........................... Economics

Science, Technology, and Society............ Natural and Physical Sciences;
Social Sciences; Humanities;
Social Studies courses

Global Connections...Geography; Culture;
Economics; Natural and
Physical Sciences; Humanities

Civic Ideals and Practices...............................History; Political Science;
Cultural Anthropology; Global Studies;
Law-Related Education; Humanities

Figure 1.4. Social Studies Conceptual Themes and Associated Courses

Although the conceptual structure for the social studies standards is solid, the performance expectations could be stated in a way that would better facilitate a concept-process curriculum and instruction. What appears to have gotten in the way is the popular notion that performance expectations have to be stated with active verbs. We have a love affair with verbs in this country. But they are such arbitrary, and often misapplied, critters in the curriculum design process. Committee members can be heard to say, "We used 'explain' five times already. How about 'articulate' on this one?"

The NCSS design committee also knew that they could not use particular performance verbs, such as *enact, design,* or *construct,* because teachers and students need choice in how knowledge is demonstrated. So, they took a fall-back position and used verbs that could be exemplified in a number of different ways, such as *compare, describe, explain,* or *interpret.* But where did these verbs come from? That's right. Everyone is dusting off *Bloom's Taxonomy of Verbs,* and we are right back to the traditional content objectives of the 1970s and early 1980s.

But in spite of the verb problem, there is something powerful in the NCSS performance expectations. Many of them are written to convey "lessons" of history, government, economics, culture, and so on. They call for understanding not of specific topics, but of the essential understandings that transfer through time and across cultures. Chart 1.4 excerpts some of the performance expectations for "Culture." Let's ignore the arbitrary verb for now and look for the important transferable idea. Can you juxtapose the words (ignoring the verb and a few other little words) in the upper-left-hand cell and create a sentence that conveys an essential understanding?

Did you come up with "Groups, societies and cultures address similar human needs and concerns in similar and different ways?" If so, you are on the way to becoming a concept-based teacher! How nice it would be if the standard statement at the top of the page read: "Social studies programs should include experiences that provide for the study of culture and cultural diversity, so the learner can *understand* that . . ."

We do want students to develop deep, conceptual understanding. And we can assess and evaluate, through performance, the student's ability to use factual content to support the conceptual understanding. Realize, however, that the juxtaposing technique mentioned above does not work for all of the performance expectations listed in the NCSS document. Take the following example: "Compare ways in which people from different cultures think about and deal with their physical environment and social conditions." We would need a few more words to complete this idea as an essential understanding.

Another problem that makes the NCSS standards a little confusing for teachers is that content and process expectations are not clearly differentiated in the performance expectations. Test yourself in Chart 1.5. For each of the performance expectations in this excerpt from "Time, Continuity and Change," decide whether the expectation is related to content understanding or process ability.

Early Grades	Middle Grades	High School
Explore and describe similarities and differences in the ways groups, societies, and cultures address similar human needs and concerns.	Explain why individuals and groups respond differently to their physical and social environments and/or changes to them on the basis of shared assumptions, values, and beliefs.	Interpret patterns of behavior reflecting values and attitudes that contribute or pose obstacles to cross-cultural understanding.
Give examples of how experiences may be interpreted differently by people from diverse cultural perspectives and frames of reference.	Explain and give examples of how language, literature, the arts, architecture, other artifacts, traditions, beliefs, values, and behaviors contribute contribute to the development and transmission of culture.	Apply an understanding of culture as an integrated whole that explains the functions and interactions of language, literature, the arts, architecture, traditions, beliefs and values, and behavior patterns.

Chart 1.4. Performance Expectations for Culture
SOURCE: Copyright © 1994 National Council for the Social Studies. Excerpted by permission.

This differentiation between process and content expectations is important in working with standards because we do not develop process ability in the same way that we develop content understandings. It is true that they must work together to reinforce each other, but the assessment criteria for content understanding and skill-based process performance differ considerably. For example, if we are assessing a student's content understanding of a Shakespearean play, then we may be interested in criteria such as depth, breadth,

Early Grades	Middle Grades	High School
Demonstrate an understanding that different people may describe the same event or situation in diverse ways, citing reasons for the differences in views.	Identify and use processes important to reconstructing and reinterpreting the past, such as using a variety of sources; providing, validating, and weighing evidence for claims; checking credibility of sources; and searching for causality.	Demonstrate that historical knowledge and the concept of time are socially influenced constructions that lead historians to be selective in the questions they seek to answer and evidence they use.
Identify and use various sources for reconstructing the past, such as documents, letters, diaries, maps, textbooks, photos, and so on.	Develop critical sensitivities such as empathy and skepticism regarding attitudes, values, and behaviors of people in different historical contexts.	Systematically employ processes of critical historical inquiry to reconstruct and reinterpret the past, such as using a variety of sources and checking their credibility, validating and weighing evidence for claims, and searching for causality.

Chart 1.5. Performance Expectations for Time, Continuity, and Change
SOURCE: Copyright © 1994 National Council for the Social Studies. Excerpted by permission.

and insight. If we are assessing technical skill in the process of writing, then we will consider criteria such as organization, development of ideas, and use of conventions.

Float the letters to each performance expectation in Chart 1.5 to see if you nailed it. P = process expectation; C = content expectation.

C	P	C
P	P	P

Economics Standards

The national standards for economics, published by the National Council on Economic Education (1997), are conceptually based. The standards state:

> The [economics] standards are primarily conceptual. They do not include important basic facts about the American and world economies. . . . Students should know some pertinent facts about the American economy, . . . and many exercises suggested in the benchmarks lead students to acquire this information. [But] the relevant facts change constantly. Conceptual standards highlight the unique contributions of economics and are enduring principles. They facilitate an emphasis on economic reasoning, encouraging students to develop the capacity to deduce conclusions from whatever facts are pertinent to the myriad of problems they will confront. . . . The standards focus on the more fundamental economic ideas and concepts that are widely shared by professional economists. (p. viii)

The content standards for economics state major, transferable ideas based on the most critical concepts of the discipline. They expand the ideas with benchmarks at Grades 4, 8, and 12. The benchmarks are also stated as transferable, conceptual understandings. Following the benchmarks, suggested performances assess student understanding of the related ideas. Figure 1.5 provides a sample from the economics design. One of the powerful aspects of this design is that the suggested activities are tied directly to the idea they illustrate. The idea is stated as a deep understanding (a transferable, conceptual idea) that requires a like performance. No fluff here!

Economics Content Standard 6

Students will understand that . . . when individuals, regions, and nations specialize in what they can produce at the lowest cost and then trade with others, both production and consumption increase.

Sample Benchmarks:

At the completion of Grade 4, students will know that
   1. Economic specialization occurs when people concentrate their production on fewer kinds of goods and services than they consume
   2. Specialization and division of labor usually increases the productivity of workers

Sample Performances:

At the completion of Grade 4, students will use this knowledge to
   1. Name several adults in the school or community who specialize in the production of a good or service (e.g., baker, law enforcement officer, teacher, etc.) and identify other goods and services that these individuals consume but do not produce for themselves.
   2. Work individually to produce a product, and then work as a member of a small group to produce the same product. Explain why more goods usually are produced when each member of the group performs a particular task in making the good.

Figure 1.5. Sample of Economic Standards, Benchmarks, and Performances, Grades K through 4

SOURCE: National Council on Economic Education. Copyright © 1997. Excerpt reprinted by permission.

Geography Standards

The national geography standards (National Geographic Research & Exploration, 1994) provide a conceptual framework to organize the content understandings. There are five conceptual themes, referred to as "essential elements": Space, Places and Regions, Physical Systems, Human Systems, and Environment and Society. A sixth element, Uses of Geography, shares the value of the geographic lens for studies related to the past, present, and future.

The standards discuss the importance of geographic inquiry leading to the development of generalizations and conclusions based on the collection, organization, and analysis of data:

> Generalizations . . . help to codify understanding. Geographic generalizations can be made using inductive reasoning or deductive reasoning. Inductive reasoning requires students to synthesize geographic information to answer questions and reach conclusions. Deductive reasoning requires students to identify relevant questions, collect and assess evidence, and decide whether the generalizations are appropriate by testing them against the real world. (National Geographic Research & Exploration, 1994, p. 44)

The concern I have with the geography standards is that even though they speak of the necessity of teaching toward conceptual generalizations, they leave the discovery of these "big ideas" up to the student and teacher. For each conceptual theme (element), topic statements list what students should "know and understand." For each of these topic statements, there is a "standard," stated as a traditional, fact-based "objective." Following the objective (Figure 1.6) are suggested "performances" that require students to apply a geographic skill to a topic—but there is no indication of the conceptual understandings that should develop as a result of the study.

We cannot assume that teachers know the conceptual ideas that should develop from these activities. The geography standards state that they followed the history standards model. Perhaps that is why these standards don't really require thinking beyond the facts or activities. I would love to see the geography standards take their excellent piece of work and carry it one step further by asking and answering the question, "What are the essential, conceptual understandings related to 'spatial distribution of population,' 'characteristics of populations,' and 'human migration' that can be learned through the eyes of geography?" Writing these understandings clearly and upfront for teachers, as the national science standards have done, would further the cause of geographic inquiry much more than would stating lower cognitive objectives and activities.

There is a clear differentiation in the geography standards between the content understandings and the geographic skills. Chart 1.6 shows a skills chart for Grades K through 4 that are actually the processes (complex performances) that a geographer would use.

Geography Standard 9

Human Systems: The Characteristics, Distribution, and Migration of Human Populations on Earth's Surface

By the end of the fourth grade, the student knows and understands

1. The spatial distribution of population
2. The characteristics of populations at different scales (local to global)
3. The causes and effects of human migration

Therefore, the student is able to

A. Describe the spatial distribution of population, as exemplified by being able to
   - Study the distribution of population on a map of the student's local community or state and suggest reasons for the patterns observed
   - Study a map of the United States showing population densities and then write an account suggesting how differences in density are related to location
   - Suggest reasons for the distribution of people on Earth . . . by comparing maps of population distribution with maps that show climate, precipitation, length of growing season, natural resources, and other physical features

---

Figure 1.6. Excerpt From National Geography Standards, Grades K-4
SOURCE: The Geography Education Standards Project: *Geography for Life: The National Geography Standards.* Copyright © 1994, National Geographic Society, Washington, DC.

Following the complex performances, "skill sets" list developmentally appropriate and precise skill abilities necessary for the complex performance. These process and skill delineations (also provided for Grades 5 through 8 and Grades 9 through 12) are excellent and provide tremendous help to classroom teachers and curriculum development committees.

One of the strongest points for the geography standards is the outstanding job with background information for the teacher. I believe that every teacher of geography should have these standards to support their instruction. The background knowledge alone would improve the teaching of geography, a critical discipline in a globally

Chart 1.6. National Geography Standards—Skills Excerpt—Grades K Through 4

Ask Geographic Questions	Acquire Geographic Information	Organize Geographic Information	Analyze Geographic Information	Answer Geographic Questions
Ask geographic questions: Where is it located? Why is it there?	Locate, gather, and process information from a variety of primary and secondary sources, including maps	Prepare maps to display geographic information	Use maps to observe and interpret geographic relationships	Present geographic information in the form of both oral and written reports accompanied by maps and graphics

1. Prepare maps to display geographic information, as exemplified by being able to
   - Map the location of places on outline maps at a variety of scales, using appropriate symbols
   - Draw sketch maps to illustrate geographic information
   - Prepare maps as a means of spatially depicting information obtained from graphs
   - Create maps that are labeled appropriately

SOURCE: The Geography Education Standards Project: *Geography for Life: The National Geography Standards.* Copyright © 1994, National Geographic Society, Washington, DC.

interdependent world. Geography has suffered sporadic classroom attention in the past. Teachers have been burdened by weak background training and either no maps or old maps. (Have you ever scrounged for a map in the old storeroom, blown the dust off, and used the marking pen to redraw current boundaries?) Geography today is much more than map and globe skills, as the national geography standards so clearly indicate.

Civics and Government Standards

The civics and government standards (November 1994) emphasize the key concepts of the discipline. The content summary and rationale for the content standards often give important conceptual ideas, but the content standards themselves, written as traditional objectives, emphasize definitional knowledge of concepts (Figure 1.7). The content load is extremely heavy and creates pressure on teachers to cover the material. The verbs *identify, describe,* and so on drive instruction toward facts and definitions rather than ideas. Although definitional knowledge of key concepts is critical, the focus for teaching and learning should be the essential ideas and understandings that incorporate the individual concepts. This brings relevance to the concepts.

So, these standards get a thumbs-up for focusing on key concepts, but to further the development of conceptual thinking and understanding, the standards could be taken a step further. As with the geography standards, greater depth could be facilitated by asking the question, "Why should students understand the concepts of 'limited and unlimited' government?" The "performances" required to demonstrate understanding of the standards contain other concepts that are important. For example, concepts such as power, law, custom, sovereign, individual rights, and popular participation can be joined in various ways to express essential, conceptual understandings that transfer. Instead of "Describe the essential characteristics of limited and unlimited governments," which is a fact-based end, the standard could read, "Understand the implications of limited and unlimited governments."

Supporting Ideas:

- Limited governments use the rule of law to restrain political power.

> *What are the essential characteristics of limited and unlimited governments?*
>
> **Content Standards:**
>
> 1. Students should be able to describe the essential characteristics of limited and unlimited governments.
>
> To achieve this standard, students should be able to
> > Describe the essential characteristics of limited and unlimited governments
> > Identify historical and contemporary examples of limited and unlimited governments and justify their classification

Figure 1.7. Civics and Government National Standards Excerpt—Grades 5 Through 8

SOURCE: Reprinted with permission, *National Standards for Civics Government*, pp. 35, 36, 79. Copyright © 1994, Center for Civic Education, 5146 Douglas Fir Rd., Calabasas, CA 91307.

- Unlimited governments use political power to restrain public action and opinion.
- Different forms of government shape social and political discourse.

The task for teachers is not to have students just know the definition of singular concepts, but to understand the fundamental principles and ideals that structure governments and societies. These conceptual understandings are developed over time through the consideration and evaluation of specific, content-based examples.

Figure 1.8 provides a stronger example of a conceptually based standard from civics and government. In this example, the standard is stated as a conceptual relationship: "Civil society is a prerequisite of limited government."

The objectives that follow the standard do require that students demonstrate deep understanding because they have to evaluate the argument presented by the standard. If you remove the introductory verbs from the objectives, you will find the supporting conceptual ideas.

Civil Society and Government. Students should be able to explain and evaluate the argument that civil society is a prerequisite of limited government.

To achieve this standard, students should be able to
> Define civil society as the sphere of voluntary personal, social, and economic relationships and organizations that, although limited by law, are not part of government (e.g., family, friendships, membership in nongovernmental organizations, participation in unions and business enterprises)
> Explain how civil society provides opportunities for individuals to associate for social, cultural, religious, economic, and political purposes
> Explain how civil society makes it possible for people individually or in association with others to bring their influence to bear on government

Figure 1.8. Civics and Government National Standards Excerpt— Grades 9 Through 12

SOURCE: Reprinted with permission, *National Standards for Civics Government*, pp. 35, 36, 79. Copyright © 1994, Center for Civic Education, 5146 Douglas Fir Rd., Calabasas, CA 91307.

Mathematics Standards

One of the earliest sets of national standards was published by the National Council of Teachers of Mathematics (1989). These curriculum and evaluation standards were developed around six basic assumptions, including the beliefs that the curriculum should

- Be conceptually oriented.

> A conceptual approach enables children to acquire clear and stable concepts by constructing meaning in the context of physical situations and allows mathematical abstractions to emerge from empirical experience. A strong conceptual framework allows skills to be acquired in ways that make sense to children . . . ; and supports the development of problem solving. (p. 17)

- Actively involve children in doing mathematics. "Young children . . . construct, modify, and integrate ideas by interacting with the physical world, materials, and other children" (p. 17). The standards use verbs such as *explore, solve, construct, discuss,* and *investigate* to encourage thoughtful participation in learning.

- Emphasize the development of children's mathematical thinking and reasoning abilities.

> The curriculum must . . . instill in students a sense of confidence in their ability to think and communicate mathematically, to solve problems, to demonstrate flexibility in working with mathematical ideas and problems, to make appropriate decisions in selecting strategies and techniques, to recognize familiar mathematical structures in unfamiliar settings, to detect patterns, and to analyze data. (pp. 17-18)

The national mathematics standards clearly support a conceptual understanding of mathematics. The discussion in the standards that requires students to make "mathematical connections" provides many examples to help teachers focus on teaching the transferable understandings of mathematics through key concepts. As one example, in Grades 5-8, "The development and exploration of patterns in Pascal's triangle can be used to illustrate relationships among counting, exponents, algebra, geometric patterns, probability, and number theory" (National Council of Teachers of Mathematics, 1989, p. 85).

The transition to a conceptual model of curriculum and instruction for mathematics, however, is hard for teachers trained in a conventional model emphasizing memorization of algorithms. The conventional model of mathematics instruction implies that understanding a concept means being able to perform the operation and apply it in an appropriate context. But students can perform an operation in a rote and thoughtless manner, and even apply it in a recognized context, but they will not really understand the concept unless they can also explain *why* the concept works in a particular situation and generalize the concept to a variety of real-world contexts.

The national mathematics standards could further help teachers by identifying clearly the integrating concepts of mathematics and by providing developmental examples of the key principles and generalizations of mathematics. This is hard work, and I have not yet seen a well-defined set of conceptual generalizations to guide mathematics instruction. But teachers need this support if we hope to reach the goal of "mathematics power" as idealized in the national standards. The mathematics standards provide many excellent examples of conceptual understandings for transfer, but state and local curriculum committees need more definitive and developmental examples of key mathematical principles and generalizations to know how to adapt conventional models of curriculum design.

The Design of State Standards

Formats for state standards vary according to the degree of specificity desired by the working committee or the legislative oversight body. In most cases, however, state committees refer to national and other state standards to design their documents. Like the national standards committees, the state committees are composed of teachers, citizens, and professionals in the field who have been trained in the objectives format of the past. In some cases, the state committees realize that they cannot write the standards at the level of specific topics. The documents would be too large. Therefore, they write standards that address the critical concepts of the discipline. But the pressure to "never separate 'know' from 'do'" too often leads to verbs linked with a topic rather than a deeper understanding. The science and technology standards for the state of Massachusetts (Figure 1.9), however, have effectively handled this problem of verbs linked to shallow knowledge. Instead of just naming a topic for the verb action, these standards name the conceptual understanding that must be demonstrated through the verb. The conceptual understandings are highlighted. These are transferable ideas based on key concepts from physical science.

Now that you have had some experience evaluating standards through the lens of a concept/process model, take a look at the generic standards in Figure 1.10, which are representative of many state standards. What kind of instruction will these standards elicit? How could these standards be adapted, or what components could be added that would shift the teaching focus from the memorization of facts to the use of facts to support increasing conceptual depth and understanding?

Learning Standards and Examples of Student Learning

Forces and Motion:

    Explore and illustrate situations that show how the position and motion of an object are judged relative to a particular frame of reference. Examine evidence that an object at rest tends to stay a rest unless acted upon by some outside force. Also, examine evidence that an object in uniform motion remains in the state of motion with constant momentum unless acted upon by an unbalanced force.

    Illustrate and describe an understanding that motion can take place in two or three dimensions. Describe an object's motion in terms of velocity or acceleration, and represent motion in various ways, including distance-time and speed-time graphs, as well as by mathematical equations and vectors.

    Explore and describe an understanding that acceleration is the rate of change of velocity, where the change may be in magnitude or direction.

    Demonstrate an understanding that constant motion in a circle requires a force to maintain it, because velocity is constantly changing.

Figure 1.9. Massachusetts Science and Technology Curriculum Framework

SOURCE: Copyright © 1995, Massachusetts Department of Education. Printed with the permission of the Massachusetts Department of Education.

State committees have done a tremendous amount of work to define critical content and processes. The examination in this book is to help those states and districts that are trying to adapt standards to a conceptually based model in order to focus both curriculum and instruction on complex thinking and deeper, conceptual structures and understanding.

Designing Local Curricula Aligned to Standards

State and local district standards intend to have students demonstrate the use and deep understanding of knowledge. They list

---

Content Standard:
"Understand the development of U.S., world, and local history."

Sample Benchmarks:
Grades K-4: Describe life in the United States before and after European contact.
Grades 5-8: Identify and explain the impact of major figures in U.S. and world history, related to significant issues, movements, and events.
Grades 9-12: Analyze significant events in U.S. history from the post–Civil War era, recognizing cause and effect, multiple causation, or the accidental as change agents.

Figure 1.10. Representative Sample of a State History Standard

sample performances that are intended to show deep understanding. What is painting the pages of many, if not most, district curricular frameworks around the country, however, looks more like the traditional "student learning objectives." But this is not surprising, because we do what we know, and we know how to write objectives. Curriculum developers draw verbs from the higher levels of *Bloom's Taxonomy* and hope that this will elicit deep understanding through whatever performance is used to "evaluate" or "analyze." But the truth is that teachers have had little training in how to do a quality assessment of students' ability to evaluate or analyze. We still lack quality models for writing tasks that will elicit "deep understanding" and complex performance. Another problem is that most of the state and national standards write performance expectations in a format that replicates traditional objectives. Many districts are using the standards formats as a guide for local curriculum development, and the traditional pattern continues. If we feel we must provide teachers with verbs to demonstrate "understanding," then Massachusetts's science and technology framework provides one of the better models because it requires a demonstration of knowledge beyond the facts. It is the statement of understanding, not the verb itself, that will draw the depth of performance.

The missing link in designing quality performance-based curricula aligned to state and national standards centers around a set of false assumptions.

False Assumption #1: State and national standards have all clearly identified the "essential understandings."

Reaction: Most state and national standards have identified essential content and skills, but assigning a verb to a topic does not ensure that teachers will lead students beyond the facts to the essential conceptual understandings. National standards, developed by discipline specialists, contain too much content to be taught effectively in the K through 12 curriculum. The only way to condense the breadth of the curriculum effectively and yet preserve the integrity of the disciplines is to ensure that the key concepts, principles, and generalizations become the focus for the selected topics of critical content. The national science standards provide a quality model that relates critical content to key concepts and conceptual understandings. This framework helps teachers bridge from facts to concepts and conceptual understandings.

False Assumption #2: We assume that teachers know how to design performances that will measure deep and essential understanding.

Reaction: Teachers have been trained to design activities that demonstrate factual knowledge and skills. Before they can design performances to measure deep understanding, they will have to learn how to identify the conceptual ideas that transcend a topic or particular set of facts. Then they will need to learn how to design performance tasks and assessment instruments that measure deeper conceptual understandings, as well as content knowledge and process abilities.

False Assumption #3: We assume that deep understanding will occur without a conceptual lens focused on a topic.

Reaction: To teach a topic without a conceptual lens to draw thinking to the higher, integration level results in a cognitively shallow study. Students and teachers cover facts but lack ideas to challenge thinking beyond the facts. I can cover the facts in a unit titled "African Nations," but if I want to raise the cognitive level, I might change the unit theme to "Changing Perspectives in African Nations." This introduction of the concept of "perspectives" forces thinking beyond the facts and draws out conceptual understandings that transfer through time and across cultures. How do changing perspectives affect political, social, and economic systems? It is at this level of thinking and understanding that the lessons of history are found and student interest is engaged.

Filling the Standards Gap
in Local Curriculum Design

If local districts and schools want to develop a coherent curriculum that uses critical content to develop the conceptual understanding of a discipline, they will design a format that shifts the instructional focus. Instead of a curriculum that assigns arbitrary verbs to topics to elicit factual information, the new design will provide

- Key concepts and increasingly sophisticated generalizations
- Conceptually based questions to elicit conceptual thinking
- Grade-level, critical content topics—listed without verbs

The processes and key skills of the discipline, provided by grade level or grade bands, convey clearly to teachers the expectations for developing the professional performances of the artist, the mathematician, or the social scientist. Teachers are given the flexibility and the license to combine process and content in any way they desire to accomplish the goals of content knowledge, conceptual understanding, and process development.

One of the better sets of district curricular frameworks I have seen in the country to convey this shift in curricular and instructional focus comes from the Lake Washington School District in Redmond, Washington. Because their frameworks exemplify a refreshing approach to curriculum design, I have included a sample in Figures 1.11 and 1.12 from two subject areas for illustration. All content-based subject areas in the Lake Washington district have the same curricular format that supports the concept-process approach. Figure 1.13 shows a sample of the Lake Washington critical content, listed by topic and level. Notice that the listing does not include verbs. This will give teachers flexibility in how they engage students with questions and process activities to gain content knowledge and conceptual understanding.

The language arts discipline from Lake Washington uses a format more suitable for these process-driven areas of study. Although they use the concept of communication to convey conceptual understandings, they also address the critical need to articulate in more detail the key processes and skills of a developmental language arts curriculum. This articulation is very important for process-driven

(text continues on p. 38)

Properties, Measurement, Scale		Thinking and Learning Scientifically	
Essential Understandings	Essential Questions	Essential Processes	Skills
Properties are qualities or quantities that characterize objects, organisms, substances, materials, events, and systems.	How do the properties of solids, liquids, and gases depend on the distance between and interaction among their particles? How does wavelength determine the type of energy in the electromagnetic spectrum? How does structure relate to function? How do the interrelationships among physical, chemical, and biological properties and processes impact a global system (e.g., ocean, atmosphere)?	Use scientific thinking to examine characteristics of political, economic, environmental, and cultural systems.	• Investigate the interaction of different systems and the consequences of their interactions. • Plan procedures to investigate hypotheses. • Select instruments and techniques to gather and synthesize research and useful information. • Evaluate effectiveness, accuracy, and reliability of instruments and techniques for specific investigations.

Figure 1.11. Science Curriculum Framework, Excerpt--Level 4, Grades 9 and 10.
SOURCE: Lake Washington School District, Redmond, Washington. Copyright © 1997. Used with permission.

Time, Place, Continuity and Change		Thinking and Learning	
Essential Understandings	Essential Questions	Essential Processes	Skills
Human and physical characteristics define regions.	How do physical characteristics define regions and their boundaries? How are regions of the United States and world related? How do the arts reflect time, place, and the human condition? How to people create places that reflect ideas, personality, and culture?	Organize investigations of historical and current issues, topics, and events.	• Identify what is known and unknown. • Formulate questions to gather information. • Identify relevant or irrelevant information. • Identify patterns and trends.

Figure 1.12. Social Studies Curriculum Framework, Excerpt—Level 2, Grades 3 Through 5
SOURCE: Lake Washington School District, Redmond, Washington. Copyright © 1997. Used with permission.

	Grade 3 *Diverse Communities*	Grade 4 *Regional Relationships*	Grade 5 *Formation of a Nation*
History	• People, places, chronological events; local city and town communities; diverse cultural communities	• Chronology and relationships: people, places, and events in Pacific NW region and Washington state; native peoples, explorers, settlers; current populations	• Chronology and relationships of key people, places, events in United States; exploration, colonization, immigration, migration; displacement of native people; revolution; westward expansion
Geography and Environment	• Human and physical features of local and diverse environments • Landforms, topography, mapping, modeling, introduction to scale • Resource management, human impact on diverse environments	• Regions of the United States: physical features, human spatial patterns • Pacific NW relative location in Pacific Rim • Use of maps, globes, and technical data and tools • State and regional resource use and management	• Relationship of environment and human spatial patterns and movement over time • Use of maps, globes, and technical data and tools • National resource use and management
Culture	• Elements and expressions of culture: local and diverse communities including historical Native Americans • Cultural beliefs and perspectives • Transmission of culture	• Elements/expressions of culture: in U.S. regions; transmission of culture • Historical and current issues related to diverse cultures in Pacific NW • Interaction: environment and culture	• Cultural diversity and issues in United States, past and present • Impact of environment on culture and culture on environment
Civics	• Citizenship role: classroom, school, community • City and local government • Teamwork and democratic process: decision making, conflict resolution	• Citizenship role: school and community • Branches of state and national governments; state constitutional rights • Teamwork and democratic process: decision making, conflict resolution	• Responsible U.S. citizenship: representative democracy • Role of foundational documents • Principles of democracy: freedom, liberty, justice, human dignity
Economics	• Meeting basic needs and wants in diverse cultures • Role of money in daily life • Impact of innovations on environments and people	• Meeting basic needs and wants in Pacific NW • Exchange of goods and ideas in Pacific Rim • Environmental-economic relations	• Impact of innovations and technology on environment • Effect of economic demands on population • Distribution of resources, wealth

Figure 1.13. Social Studies Critical Content, Excerpt--Level 2, Grades 3 Though 5

SOURCE: Lake Washington School District, Redmond, Washington. Copyright © 1996. Used with permission.

disciplines such as language arts (reading, writing, listening, viewing, and speaking); mathematics; physical education; and skill-based business courses.

Mathematics is both skill driven and concept driven, so the curriculum framework for mathematics must address both components with rigor. Mathematics is taught as skill-based process. The teaching of conceptual understanding is generally weak in U.S. mathematics curricula. We tend to "do" mathematics rather than understand the conceptual foundations of mathematics. Perhaps that is why so many students have difficulty relating to mathematics. They do not understand the conceptual structure—nor do they know *why* algorithms and functions "work" in different contexts. We need to call on university instructors to broaden and deepen mathematics education for teachers. Lake Washington is attempting to address the deeper conceptual understanding of mathematics through the use of conceptually based essential questions (Figure 1.14).

Lake Washington, and any other district that takes on the design of concept/process curricula, has a big job with staff development. We can design the most sophisticated curriculum, but if we fall down in the training of our teachers, high ideals will drop to dust. Lake Washington knows that teachers need to be able to explain how concept/process curricula and instruction differ from traditional models. They need the expertise to design conceptually based units of study around the designated critical content by drawing essential understandings, questions, and processes and skills from the district frameworks. Congratulations to Lake Washington for the exemplary work to date. They will continue to refine their documents as they gain new insights on concept-process curricula, but even at this point in the development, they provide a valuable model to stir the minds and hearts of other districts.

Lake Washington chose to let schools and grade levels design their own units of study aligned with the district frameworks. All classes are networked with computers, which allows sharing of units across the district. Another effective strategy used by many districts is to design core units of study at the district level through representative teacher teams. This is especially useful where teachers in individual schools may not have the time or technology to facilitate site-based unit design.

Figure 1.15 shares a quality example of a district-level core unit for social studies that was developed by teachers in Plainville, Connecticut.

Essential Understandings	Essential Questions	Essential Processes	Skills
Number Sense and Spatial Relationships • Transformations of geometric shapes include reflections, translations, rotations, and dilations. • Geometric transformations relate properties of various shapes to similarity and congruence.	**Number Sense and Spatial Relationships** • How do properties of shapes establish congruence or similarity? • How do attributes of shapes change or not change when the shapes are dissected? • How are proportions used to describe relationships between similar shapes?	**Reason Mathematically** • Extract, interpret, compare, and contrast information from a variety of sources (e.g., printed materials, models, graphs, tables). • Find or create counter-examples. • Form arguments to justify and verify reasonableness of interpretations, predictions, and conclusions.	**Number Sense and Spatial Relationships** • Use attributes of shape and size to describe two- and three-dimensional shapes. • Construct geometric models and scale drawings using a variety of appropriate tools. • Use compass, straight edge, and computer software to create geometric constructions. • Represent 3-D objects in 2-D. • Classify figures in terms of congruence and similarity.

Critical Content

Number Sense
- Structure of number systems
- Real numbers
- Operations with real numbers
- Properties of real numbers
- Ratio and proportion
- Powers and roots

Spatial Relationships
- Attributes and properties of 2-D and 3-D shapes
- Transformations: reflection, rotation, translation, dilation
- Symmetry, similarity, congruence
- Coordinate systems
- Tools: compass, protractor, straight edge, computer software

Figure 1.14. Mathematics Curriculum Framework, Excerpt—Level 4, Grades 9 and 10
SOURCE: Lake Washington School District, Redmond, Washington. Copyright © 1997. Used with permission.

Subject Area: Social Studies

Concept	Grade Level	Unit Theme	Essential Understandings	Essential Questions
Cultural Unity and Diversity	1	Cultural Unity and Diversity in Families	- Culture influences the daily lives of families. - Family celebrations express the traditions of a culture. - Geographic locations influence how families live. - Different climates influence the types of recreation. - Family members may live in different locations. - Distance between family members may require different forms of communication. - Families change over time. - Economic and social changes create new roles and responsibilities. - Families meet needs and wants in different ways. - Families express their heritage through dance, literature, art, and music.	- How does culture influence holidays and traditions? - What holidays do you celebrate with your family? - What traditions does your family celebrate? - How does geographic location influence traditions? - How does geographic location affect the daily lives of families? - What is your family heritage? - Why is the acceptance of different traditions important? - How does your family meet its needs and wants? - How has your family changed over time? - How do you communicate with family members who live in another place?

Content Web:

Literature
• Multicultural authors and stories
• Family stories
• Folklore

Economy
• Needs/wants
• Parents' work
• Allowances

Geography
• Geographic location of family members
• Meeting needs in different environments

Culture
• Customs/traditions
• Holidays
• Similarities/differences
• Food, clothing, music
• Different traditions

History
• Family tree
• Heritage
• Celebrating diversity

Art/Music
• Family songs
• Cultural diversity of art and music

(Cultural Unity and Diversity in Families)

Figure 1.15. Unit Plan Example, Grade Level 1, Page 1

SOURCE: Plainville Community School District, Plainville, Connecticut: Joanne Pudlik and Dianne Smith. Used with permission.

Notice that this unit uses the conceptual lens of Cultural Unity and Diversity to integrate the study. Generalizations are listed in a column as "Essential Understandings," which are the focus of instruction. These understandings transfer across time and across cultures. The content topics shown around the web provide the foundation to support the mental bridging to conceptual understanding. Districts can choose to format concept-process curricula in different ways, but they will want to include the critical components: critical content, key concepts, essential understandings (generalizations), essential questions, and discipline-based processes and skills.

Figure 1.16 shows a content planning page from another grade level in the Plainville social studies curriculum. Notice that the essential understandings are more sophisticated at this level.

Lake Washington and Plainville teachers and administrators worked to address the "gap" in standards as they aligned their curriculum. They extrapolated key generalizations—conceptual ideas that could transfer to other situations—from their topics of study. They wrote the generalizations following the kinds of procedures outlined in Chapter 3 of this book. Teachers from districts around the country who have been involved in developing concept-process curricula have discovered powerful connections within and across disciplines. They recognize that traditional curriculum and instruction models often fall short because they fail to challenge students' thinking beyond the facts. When students learn to think beyond the facts, they are able to see patterns and connections of old knowledge and new knowledge; they transfer understandings to other situations; and they systematically build conceptual depth and sophistication.

Summary

The traditional design of a curriculum, which values memorization more than the development of complex thinking ability, did not come into question when business operated with an industrial model that called for factory workers who could follow orders, carry out repetitive tasks with little thought, and work in relative isolation. But business has changed drastically, and education is adapting to meet the need for workers who can identify and solve complex problems, think independently as well as in team situations, and exhibit the characteristics of leaders no matter what their job in an organization.

Subject Area: Social Studies

Concept	Grade Level	Unit Theme	Essential Understandings	Essential Questions
Cultural Unity and Diversity	4	Regions of the U.S.	- Survival depends on adaptations to the environment. - A lack of available resources can change the density of populations. - Changing economic conditions can create shifts in immigration patterns. - Legislative decisions reflect social and economic issues. - Celebrations and traditions reinforce cultural identity. - The arts of a region communicate cultural traditions, and historic events. - Economic need can lead to advancements in transportation and communication systems. - Technological advancement require increased job skills for workers. - Different cultural groups in a region have different degrees of power and influence.	- How do cultures develop and change? - How are the beliefs and practices of cultures related to time, location, and events? - How are cultures similar in how they meet their needs? How are they different? - How do cultures express their beliefs and ways of thinking, knowing, and doing? - What are the common components that organize and maintain society? - How does the exchange of ideas and innovations impact culture? - How do physical characteristics define regions and their boundaries?

Content Web:

Mathematics
- Data charts
- Currency
- Conversion tables
- Latitude/longitude
- Measurement
- Celsius/Fahrenheit
- Patterns
- Problem solving

Science
- Physical environment
- Resources
- Survival/adaptation
- Shelter
- Populations

Regions of the United States

Culture
- Major cultural influences in regions; native/immigrants
- Impact of environment
- Traditions, food, music
- Assimilation issues
- Cultural adaptation
- Jobs
- Schooling

History
- Settlement
- Statehood
- Immigration patterns
- Melting pot vs. salad bowl
- Conflict

Geography
- Product, political, physical maps
- Location of states and regions
- Comparative geographic data

Figure 1.16. Unit Plan Example, Grade Level 4, Page 1

SOURCE: Plainville Community School District, Plainville, Connecticut: Crystal Collins and Joyce Goldberg. Used with permission.

We are living in an increasingly complex world. Global interdependence calls for broadened social and political knowledge and skills. This recognition, as well as international comparisons of educational achievement, has led to the development of national academic standards in the United States over the past decade.

A sampling of these national standards, through a concept-process perspective, reveals a recognition of the importance of conceptual knowledge related to critical content, as well as discipline-based process abilities. The national science standards provide the most comprehensive and sound treatment of a discipline from the conceptual design perspective. Local districts can use the science standards as a model for writing "supporting ideas" (essential conceptual understandings) for their content-based disciplines, as well as key processes and skills. Teachers need this kind of clear and focused guidance if we are to be successful in actually raising standards. Raising academic content standards rests on the ability to simultaneously raise thinking standards.

Chapter 2 considers the coherence of curriculum design for K through 12 education by looking more closely at the meaning and implications of a concept-process curriculum in the context of a systems design. A systems design for a curriculum plans deliberately for the content and process sides of a curriculum. There is the expectation that both components will systematically show increasing sophistication as students progress through the grades. The content and process components interact in instruction and assessment; but in curricular frameworks and learning plans, they also have their own criteria.

໑ 2 ໑

Ensuring Coherence in Curriculum

What Is a Coherent Curriculum?

In 1995, the Association for Supervision and Curriculum Development (ASCD) published their yearbook, *Toward a Coherent Curriculum.* This collection of articles, edited by James Beane, presents thoughtful discourse by leading educators on the meaning of coherence in the curriculum. Beane states, "A 'coherent' curriculum is one that holds together, that makes sense as a whole; and its parts, whatever they are, are unified and connected by that sense of the whole" (Beane, 1995, p. 3). Beane ties the attributes of "a sense of purpose, unity, relevance and pertinence" (p. 4) to the idea of a coherent curriculum. He proposes that a curriculum cannot be coherent if students do not realize the relevance of the study to their everyday lives.

Although I agree with most of Beane's perspectives, there is one issue I question. Beane contends that designing the curriculum around separate subjects in school is artificial and fragments the desire for coherence. He discusses the movement toward various forms of integration and the use of broad themes that have significance in helping students understand the human condition and our world. He expresses support for the use of significant themes to organize learning experiences for children, but he elaborates on the political and philosophical problems inherent in the choice of themes.

It is apparent that the traditional demarcation between subjects has been intense over the years. ("I don't have to spell correctly, Mom. That's a geography paper!") At the secondary level, traditional structures force teachers to condense instruction into 45- or 50-minute chunks as students do the "cognitive shift shuffle." Teaching isolation means that instructors often know little of each other's curriculum and may care even less. We are understandably passionate about our own subject.

But to do away with the disciplines and move to "themes" that call on information in a more fluid manner is a very complex curriculum design feat, and a quantum leap for teachers who have been working within the structure of disciplines. Even if we were to reach agreement on a "coherent" presentation of centering themes drawn from the shared concerns of the larger society, how could we ensure integrity of instruction through the grades related to the key concepts and principles that form the foundation of each discipline? How would we support elementary teachers so that their instructional activities reflect a balance of discipline-based ideas and questions? And how would we prevent the gaps of critical content and conceptual knowledge that would surely appear if some teachers greatly deemphasized or ignored one of the disciplines because they had greater passions or background in certain subjects? And finally, how would we ensure a balanced development in the ability to perform as an artist, a geographer, or a scientist if we did not relate their abilities to discipline-based work in a systematic way?

A Systems Design for Coherence

Let me share another perspective on the idea of a coherent curriculum—a perspective drawn from the systems design for curriculum presented in Figure 2.1.

A systems design for curriculum is coherent, balanced, and systematically develops sophistication in knowledge, understanding, and the ability to perform. A systems design addresses four critical components: (a) the student outcomes (what students should know, understand, and be able to do based on the identified knowledge, skills, and abilities they will need as "educated" and successful citizens in the 21st century); (b) the critical content, key concepts, and

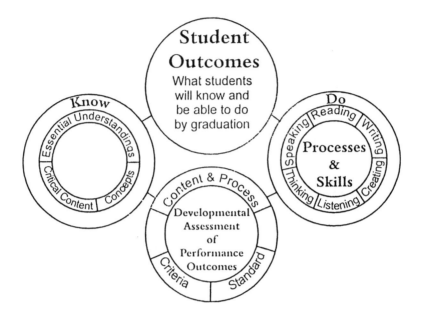

Figure 2.1. Systems Design for Curriculum

essential understandings that frame the knowledge base of different areas of study; (c) the major process and skill abilities that ensure quality performance; and (d) quality assessments for measuring standards-driven performance.

We need to discuss the balance between "know" and "do" in curriculum design. Some people state that we should never separate know and do—that content should always be presented along with a performance in curriculum frameworks. Although this statement helps educators realize the importance of taking knowledge to the doing level, I think it also creates confusion. Many state and district standards, and curriculum frameworks, present a list of know and do statements that are all driven by verbs. Teachers tend to focus on the verb and often fail to differentiate whether or not the standard is calling for content understanding, a process demonstration, or a combination. Documents that clearly differentiate process-based from content-based standards reflect the awareness that there is a difference between process and content, and that each has its own inherent criteria for instruction and assessment. In most cases, the national standards recognize and highlight these differences.

Quality curriculum designs balance content understanding and process expectations. They realize that we have two major strands in K through 12 curriculum and instruction; that know and do work together but also have their own requirements. Assigning an action verb to a topic usually focuses the study to the information level, and the instructor is left to teach beyond the facts with little support (e.g., "Identify the causes of the Civil War"). Answering the question "Why identify the causes . . . ?" leads to deeper understandings, which should provide focus for instruction.

We have two goals in a systems design for curriculum. One is to ensure that students develop process and skill abilities developmentally as they move through the grades; another is to ensure that students develop an increasing fund of critical content knowledge and conceptual understanding. If we are going to achieve these goals (which require different forms of instruction), then we need to be clear in our expectations for each strand in the layout of the curriculum. This planning is the basis for a coherent curriculum.

We have worked for many years in this country to develop the process and skill abilities of students. One thing should be clear from the "whole language" experience—whenever we stray too far from a structure for curriculum and instruction, we lose ground. We need to maintain that critical balance between too much structure, which can shut down and stifle thinking, and too little structure, which is inefficient in the teaching-learning process. Time is precious. Curricular and instructional planning needs to be focused and systematic, yet provide flexibility for instruction.

When I refer to essential understandings in the systems design, I am talking about the key principles and generalizations that develop from the fact base. They are essential because they are the deeper lessons of history, science, art, and so on. They are the "big ideas" that transfer through time and across cultures. Essential understandings are the foundational ideas on which students build increasing conceptual depth and understanding. Essential understandings are "deep understandings."

Deep and Essential Understandings

Caine and Caine (1997), in *Education on the Edge of Possibility*, state that "meaningful learning includes both 'deep' and 'felt' meanings."

They define deep meaning as "whatever drives us and governs our sense of purpose. Deep meaning is an [intrinsic] source of energy that spurs inquiry (pp. 111-112).

Felt meaning, according to the Caines,

> is an almost visceral sense of relationship, an unarticulated sense of connectedness that ultimately culminates in insight. An insight, an "aha!" is a gestalt. It is the coming together of thoughts and ideas and senses and impressions and emotions. . . . Genuine understanding links thought and feeling, mind and body. (p. 113)

I understand deep meaning, as described by Caine and Caine, as the personal, emotional, and value-driven component in the process of constructing deep understandings. The unfolding of felt meaning, to the level of insight, culminates in a summary of deep and essential understanding. Engaging student activity and performance are critical to the development and sharing of deep understanding.

David Perkins (1992) quotes Jerome Bruner's statement (1973) that the person who understands something is capable of "going beyond the information given." Perkins provides a sample of "understanding performances" that could demonstrate both knowledge and the ability to use that knowledge in the spirit of going beyond:

> *Explanation.* Explain in your own words what it means to go at a constant speed in the same direction and what sorts of forces might divert an object.
>
> *Exemplification.* Give fresh examples of the law at work. For instance, identify what forces divert the paths of objects in sports, in steering cars, in walking.
>
> *Application.* Use the law to explain a phenomenon not yet studied. For instance, what forces might make a curve ball curve?
>
> *Justification.* Offer evidence in defense of the law; formulate an experiment to test it. For instance, to see the law at work, how can you set up a situation as little influenced by friction and gravity as possible?
>
> *Comparison and Contrast.* Note the form of the law and relate it to other laws. What other laws can you think of that say that something stays constant unless such-and-such?

Contextualization. Explore the relationship of this law to the larger tapestry of physics; how does it fit into the rest of Newton's laws, for example? Why is it important? What role does it play?

Generalization. Does the form of this law disclose any more general principles about physical relationships, principles also manifested in other laws of physics? For instance, do all laws of physics say in one way or another that something stays constant unless such-and-such? (p. 77)

Perkins questions curriculum documents that frame goals with the language, "Students will *understand* . . . ," and he wonders how we can tell whether students have really attained understanding. A goal can ask that students understand Newton's laws. But whether students recite the laws, write algebraic translations, or carry out a few manipulations with the laws, the actions could be rote or "canned," with little understanding (p. 76).

I do not think the problem lies in the use of the verb *understand*, however. The problem lies in naming the topic "Newton's laws" rather than citing a desired essential understanding. If we state the objective as "Students will understand that the momentum of an object influences its trajectory," then teachers have a clear conceptual idea toward which they can teach. This idea can be demonstrated through the kinds of understanding performances shared by Perkins.

When we dictate to teachers the kinds of performance they must use with students to elicit understanding (explain, justify, etc.), then we cause them to focus more on the verb than on the idea to be demonstrated. We want teachers to focus on the idea by asking, "How can I engage students to ensure the demonstration of this understanding?" By specifying a particular verb, we rob teachers of the opportunity to engage students creatively with the kinds of performance they (or their students) wish to use for the demonstration.

Curriculum developers may assume that teachers know the essential understandings related to a topic. My experience has been that unless teachers consciously identify these understandings, they focus on the fact-based content as the endpoint in instruction, and the conceptual level of understanding usually is not addressed.

Teachers have been well trained in the traditional model of curriculum design (institutionalized as booklets of objectives during the behaviorist era), which emphasizes fact-based memorization and skill building. How, then, can we assume that teachers know how to identify the key concepts and conceptual ideas underlying the fact base? Where have they been trained to generalize knowledge and ideas beyond the facts?

National and state frameworks consistently have a standard that says, "Students will understand the concepts and principles of [science, social studies, mathematics, etc.]." The traditional and prevalent models of curriculum design list a myriad of topics and facts to be learned (covered), but they fail to emphasize key concepts and principles. This omission creates a missing link in the curriculum and implementation designs of some national standards and most state and district standards.

Concepts and Process in Curriculum Design

Dealing With the "Know" in Curriculum Design

A systems design for curriculum raises the standard for what students should know. The curriculum design framing the past schooling of most adults defined what students should know by topics and related facts. Traditional objectives asked students to "list," "define," "identify," and "explain" important, fact-based information.

But this model of linking arbitrary verbs to topics is limiting and antiquated for the information age, where knowledge is expanding exponentially and the ability to process a large amount of information at abstract levels of thinking becomes more critical each year. If we are to develop the thinking abilities of students systematically, then we need to move from a solely topic-centered to an idea-centered model of curriculum design.

The difference between a topic-centered and an idea-centered curriculum/instruction model is the difference between memorizing facts related to the American Revolution and developing and sharing ideas related to the concepts of freedom and independence as a result of studying the American Revolution. It is the difference between viewing the O.J. Simpson trial and drawing insights into the concept of justice from discussions of the trial. It is the difference between the facts of the Alaska oil spill and an understanding of the importance of environmental sustainability. Finally, it is the difference between the construction of mathematical angles and the knowledgeable application of geometric form to ensure architectural strength in design.

Topic-centered curricula focus heavily on the memorization of facts and assume the development of deeper ideas. Idea-centered curricula focus on deeper, conceptual ideas and use facts to support the understandings. Facts are viewed not only as critical for building content knowledge but also as tools for gaining insight into the conceptual ideas that transfer across time and cultures.

For example, if we study the topic of the American Revolution, we can learn specific facts and information related to this period of history. But if we look at the American Revolution through the lens of "dependence/independence," then we can define transferable lessons of history that students can apply in their future study. Following are some lessons of history that could be drawn from the study of the American Revolution through the conceptual lens of dependence/independence:

- Economic need can create a dependence of one nation upon another.
- Social, economic, or political oppression often leads to conflict or revolution.
- A nation's desire for political or economic freedom and independence may facilitate alliances with other nations.

These lessons of history, appropriate for a middle elementary grade level, are essential understandings that transcend time and cultures. Concept-process teachers clearly identify and teach toward these transferable ideas. Specific topics become the building blocks for developing increasingly sophisticated ideas.

Every content-based discipline has a core of conceptual, essential understandings. In this age of knowledge overload, students need a mental schema to pattern and sort information. As they progress through the grades, students build conceptual structures in the brain as they relate new examples to past learnings. This means that teachers, in writing curricula, need to identify conceptual ideas, often stated as essential understandings, that are developmentally appropriate for the age level of their students. Conceptual understandings become more sophisticated from elementary through secondary and postsecondary schools. I would not generally expect to see,

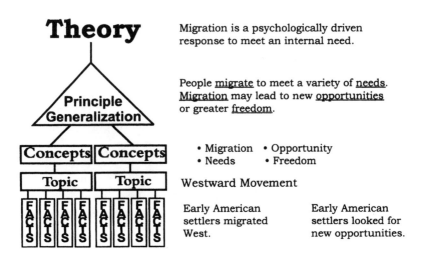

Figure 2.2. Structure of Knowledge Example

in a concept-based (idea-centered) curriculum, the same essential understandings at the high school level that I see in the elementary curriculum.

Identifying and writing essential understandings is not an easy task. It requires learning a new skill—thinking beyond the topic and facts to the important, transferable ideas. A first step is to understand how knowledge is structured, as presented in Chapter 1, Figure 1.1. Let's review the example in Figure 2.2 to understand how concept-based curriculum and instruction differs from topic based.

How do the topics and facts that we teach relate to critical concepts, principles, and generalizations? In Figure 2.2, Gayle Jones, a fourth-grade teacher, works with the topic of Early American settlers. She knows that students will learn critical facts related to the study, such as "Early American settlers looked for new opportunities and greater personal freedom" and "Early American settlers migrated to the West."

But Mrs. Jones also knows that this topic provides the opportunity to help students understand some critical concepts that they can use again and again as they meet new examples throughout their schooling: migration, needs, freedom, and opportunity.

Mrs. Jones puts different concepts together in her planning to form some of the key conceptual ideas that will drive her teaching.

These conceptual ideas are the key generalizations that go beyond the specific facts of Early American settlers to the "transferable knowledge" level.

Mrs. Jones identifies two key generalizations:

- People migrate to meet a variety of needs.
- Migration may lead to enhanced opportunity or greater personal freedom.

These are important ideas for students to understand because they can be applied across many examples to deepen conceptual understanding. For example, in the generalization, "People migrate to meet a variety of needs," neither the migrating people nor their specific needs are identified. The idea can be applied to different migrating groups throughout time and across cultures. As students and the teacher ask questions about each new example, such as "Why did the Haitians migrate to America in the 1980s?" or "Why did the Russians migrate to America after the end of the Cold War?" they develop deeper understandings and greater conceptual insight. New generalizations are formed to express the insights. A fourth grader would understand the generalizations cited previously, but by the time a student is in high school, the generalization should be more sophisticated, such as "Governments set immigration quotas to maintain social, political, and economic balance in a society."

The top level in the structure of knowledge is "theory." Theories are conceptual ideas that beg to be proven. Theories present provocative ideas that draw multiple perspectives, deep discussion, and a research base. This book does not address theories in the design schema in order to keep the focus on the first stage of critical work— learning how to organize the content of the curriculum around key concepts, generalizations, and principles.

The difference between generalizations and principles is that principles are key conceptual relationships that are always true and have significant roles in a discipline, such as Boyle's Law in science. They stand the test of eternal time, they will never change, and they are cornerstones for understanding and applying the knowledge of a discipline.

Generalizations, on the other hand, may fail to hold up over time and across all examples. They must always be tested for truth.

If a generalization is an important conceptual idea that is generally true, then it is legitimate to teach the idea with a qualification, such as "often," "may," or "can." If a generalization is true across all examples, then qualifiers are not used.

Principles and generalizations are written in identical form. They are both statements of important conceptual relationship. The differences lie in their link to truth and their significance to the foundations of the discipline.

In curriculum design and instruction, a major task at this time is to address clearly the key concepts and generalizations (essential understandings) related to the critical content of our disciplines. Figure 2.3 provides a sample of key concepts related to a variety of disciplines.

There are some key points to consider as we review these discipline-based concepts:

Each set of concepts structures the content of the particular discipline. For example, if we talk about organisms, or cells, we are obviously in the field of science. It is because of this discipline structure that we should plan thoughtfully when designing integrated curricula. We must exercise care not to destroy the conceptual integrity of the disciplines.

Some of the concepts are very broad, such as "change," "interdependence," or "system," and can be applied across any discipline and a wide variety of topics. These can be referred to as "macroconcepts." Macroconcepts, which are highlighted in Figure 2.3, work well as conceptual lenses for integrated, interdisciplinary units of study because of their ability to cross a variety of topics in different disciplines. Although some concepts cut across the disciplines, they are exemplified in different contexts. Chapter 3 will demonstrate how to use a conceptual lens for integrating units of study.

Because the field of language arts is process and skill based, it is the component of literature/media that provides the content base for drawing out the concepts. The concepts for literature/media are what we have always referred to as the "themes" of literature, or they are concepts related to the study of literature as a discipline (e.g., character, plot, setting). Concepts are nouns that frame topics drawn from content study. Therefore, concepts are found in the content of

Science	Social Studies	Literature
Order	Conflict/cooperation	Time
Organism	Patterns	Space
Population	Populations	**Interactions**
Systems	**Systems**	**Change**
Change	**Change/continuity**	Beliefs/values
Evolution	Culture	Motivation
Cycle	Evolution	Conflict/cooperation
Interaction	Civilization	Perceptions
Energy/matter	Migration/immigration	**Patterns**
Equilibrium	**Interdependence**	**Systems**

Mathematics	Music	Visual Art
Number	Rhythm	Rhythm
Ratio	Melody	Line
Proportion	Harmony	Color
Symmetry	Tone	Value
Probability	Pitch	Shape
Pattern	Form	**Pattern**
Order	Tempo	Texture
Quantification	Timbre	**Form**
System	**Pattern**	Space
		Angle

Figure 2.3. Sample Subject Area Concepts
NOTE: Macroconcepts are in bold type.

> A **concept** is an organizing idea; a mental construct . . .
>
> Timeless
> Universal
> Abstract and broad
> Represented by 1 or 2 words
> Examples share common attributes

Figure 2.4. Definition and Attributes of a Concept

subject areas rather than in the process work of disciplines. Sometimes, verbs are derived from a conceptual noun base (e.g., "evolves," from the concept of "evolution"). Figure 2.4 shows the definition and characteristics of a concept.

By definition, a concept is a mental construct, an organizing idea that categorizes a variety of examples. Although the examples may differ in context, they have common attributes. Symmetry, for example, is a concept that is exemplified by many different examples, but all examples display the attribute of "balance." Concepts also meet the following criteria:

Timeless—The concepts that frame the content of our disciplines will always be with us. We have always had the concept of conflict, for example, and we will always have it. What changes through time are the specific examples. This quality of timelessness is one reason that concepts make excellent organizers for a content base that is continually shifting, expanding, and growing in complexity. We can remain grounded to the conceptual structure of knowledge yet have some flexibility with the specific topics.

Universal—Concepts are the same across the world. The specific examples may differ from culture to culture, but the concepts are universal. In an increasingly multicultural society, the ability to draw cross-cultural examples to understand concepts is a helpful tool.

Abstract and broad—By nature, concepts are abstract and broad in order to provide for a variety of examples. We have been trained in education to believe that abstract is "fuzzy," and specific is better, because it is more clearly tested. But what are we testing—

memorization of specific facts as our goal, or the ability to use facts to support the expression of conceptual understanding? Look at the two examples following. Which has greater clarity and specificity? Which has greater intellectual power? How can we address both examples in our instruction?

> *Fact:* The Montana Freemen had a standoff with the U.S. government because they felt that their constitutional rights had been violated.
>
> *Generalization (conceptual idea that transfers):* "Individuals and groups react to issues and events based on their values and worldviews." (Concepts are underlined.)

The following chapters will share additional examples of key concepts and generalizations for different subject areas.

Dealing With the "Do" in Curriculum Design

A systems design for curriculum also raises the standard for what students will be able to do in their performances. The traditional design of curriculum, at its peak during the behaviorist era, defined what students should be able to do by listing discrete skills for process categories such as reading, writing, listening, and speaking. The idea was that if teachers taught the required skills at each grade level in a very direct fashion, then these skills would assuredly coalesce into a quality reader, writer, listener, and speaker. But instruction became a flurry of pencil-and-paper ditto drills on isolated skill bits.

Today, we see multiple curriculum models developing for language arts that range from very specific skill delineations to elusive descriptions of performance. But what kind of curriculum model will provide a balance in the delineation of skills?

Skills can be written with different degrees of specificity. We can depict this "nested" hierarchy through an example from the reading area:

- Complex process (performance)

- Reads a variety of literary materials with fluency and comprehension

- Performance indicators
  - Applies reading skills and strategies appropriate for the type of material
  - Constructs meaning by connecting ideas within text and to prior knowledge
- Discrete skills
  - Decodes unknown words, and blends sounds left to right
  - Uses context to aid word recognition and comprehension
  - Identifies the main ideas in text material

Once the complex performances have been identified, developmentally appropriate "performance indicators" are defined for each grade level or grade band. A curriculum design question will be the degree of specificity to bring to the indicators. Less is better than more. There needs to be enough specificity in the indicators to convey clearly what the performance will look like at the different developmental levels. Teaching materials provide the detail of discrete skills. We need to teach discrete skills, but our focus should remain on the performance we hope to elicit. The performance indicators provide the target.

For years in education, we have lamented that middle school and high school teachers, in areas other than English, do not generally see their job as teaching and assessing the language arts within their subject. We have wanted to integrate the language arts across the curriculum. I think that the problem has been that we have not approached, in our curriculum designs, the particular nuances of language arts process and skill as exhibited in the performances of the professional scientist, artist, and so on. The national standards in each discipline have addressed this problem quite well. The standards provide a wealth of information on the desired complex performances and skills for the scientist, the mathematician, the artist, and so on.

Heidi Hayes-Jacobs (1997) states that we can improve our students' ability to perform if we think of how the professionals perform in their work. What kinds of complex performances define the scientist, the artist, the mathematician? I agree with this direction for thinking about relevant processes and skills.

Science	*The Arts*
Use scientific inquiry to design and conduct scientific investigations:	Apply the creative process using arts knowledge and skills to reason and solve problems:
• Identify questions and concepts that guide scientific investigations. • Use technology and mathematics to improve investigations and communications. • Formulate and revise scientific explanations and models using logic and evidence. • Recognize and analyze alternative explanations and models. • Communicate and defend a scientific argument.	• Gather and process information through the senses. • Examine an art product using a critique process. • Generate solutions to problems using creativity and imagination. • Create artistic models to represent ideas. • Use common concepts in the arts to express ideas with image, sound, action, and movement.

Figure 2.5. Comparing Complex Performances and Performance Indicators
SOURCE: National Research Council (1996).

To design appropriate structures for complex performances, we need cutting-edge curriculum designs that will use national standards in each content area to define the broad performances of the professional in major areas such as Critical and Creative Thinking, Communicating, Producing, and Participating. Figure 2.5 shows examples of complex performances that might show up under each of these categories for the scientist and the artist.

Figure 2.6 shows an excerpt from the social studies curriculum framework of the Lake Washington School District, Redmond, Washington. This excerpt shows only how processes are defined as complex performances (listed in the left-hand column) under the process heading of Thinking and Learning. To the right of each complex performance, the matrix shows the performance indicators (broader

Social Studies Key Processes and Skills—Thinking and Learning					
Key Processes	Skills				
	Level 1	Level 2	Level 3	Level 4	Level 5
• Investigate historical and current issues, topics, and events.	• Identify what is known and unknown about an issue or topic. • Identify problems, patterns, and changes. • Formulate and ask questions that lead to new learning.	• Identify what is known and unknown about an issue or topic. • Identify problems, patterns, trends, and changes. • Formulate questions to gather information. • Identify relevant or irrelevant information. • Trace the origin, development, and impact of ideas and inventions.	• Identify problems, patterns, trends, and changes. • Formulate questions to conduct inquiry. • Identify relevant or irrelevant information. • Assess the impact of ideas and technological developments on society and the environment.	• Formulate questions and connect ideas to create new knowledge. • Investigate trends, relationships, and changes in political, economic, social, and environmental systems. • Relate historical events to the present and future. • Analyze historical, social, and geographic developments.	• Design complex questions to develop deeper knowledge and understanding of topics, issues, and events. • Analyze relationships among social, political, economic, and environmental systems. • Seek solutions to current social and environmental issues.

Figure 2.6. Excerpt From Key Processes and Skills for Social Studies

SOURCE: Lake Washington School District, Redmond, Washington. Copyright 1997. Used with permission.

skills) for five levels (grade bands), K through 12. Other pages not shown here delineate complex performances and developmental performance indicators for other headings: Collaborating, Producing, Communicating, and Participating. These general listings could each be broken down into more discrete skill delineations, but I think the presented level of detail conveys enough information to suggest the requisite skills. This format for defining complex performances and skills is used across all subject areas in the Lake Washington curriculum and takes on the particular nuances of each discipline.

Summary

Yes, a coherent curriculum is one that holds together, that makes sense as a whole, and where the parts are unified and connected by the sense of the whole" (Beane, 1995, p. 3). But a coherent curriculum also fosters through the grades, in a deliberate and systematic design, increasing sophistication in critical content knowledge, conceptual understanding, and complex performance abilities. The current emphasis on meeting national and state standards requires thoughtful planning in curriculum design. We cannot afford to do dinosaurs and rain forests at three different grade levels. We need to use the precious time in schools to maximum advantage. This does not mean that we cannot do thematic, integrated units or bring relevance and active student engagement into the learning process. But it does signal the need for coherent curricular plans that achieve the desired outcomes for students—outcomes that are based on the realities of living, learning, and working in the 21st century, as well as the mandates of discipline-based standards and assessments.

To develop increasing sophistication in critical content knowledge, decisions have to be made about what is truly "critical." In which topics must students engage in order to truly understand the discipline? What should students know in order to progress to the next level of learning? Correlating critical content topics at each grade level with key concepts to be developed shows the conceptual structure of the different disciplines. Once the topics and key concepts are identified for the content subjects (social studies, health, science), then broader themes can be developed to allow integrated treatment of critical content where feasible.

To develop increasing sophistication in conceptual understanding, two things need to occur in curriculum design:

1. Concepts need to "spiral" through the grade levels. We might study the concept of "organism" in science at Grades 1, 7, and 11, but the examples of study might be "Life Cycles of Organisms" at Grade 1, "Diversity and Adaptation of Organisms" at Grade 7, and "Evolution, Behavior, and Interdependence of Organisms" at Grade 11. The concept remains the same, but the topics change. Students develop increasing conceptual understanding related to the concept of organism as they meet new examples.

2. Out of the topics and unit themes studied through the grades, generalizations (essential understandings) are identified in the planning process. The goal is to teach students to think conceptually. This will occur in classrooms only if teachers identify and teach toward conceptual ideas. Chapter 3 shows teachers how to design integrated, interdisciplinary units of instruction that have a conceptual focus.

◖ 3 ◗

Designing Integrated, Interdisciplinary Units: A General Academic Model

A Conceptually Driven Model

Instructional units that shed a conceptual lens on a topic of study force thinking to the integration level. It is the conceptual focus that achieves this goal of integrated curriculum. Without the focus concept, we are merely "coordinating" facts and activities to a topic, and we fail to reach higher-level curricular and cognitive integration.

Take history instruction as an example. We say that by learning about the past, students will understand the future and see the patterns and connections of history. But if the curriculum does not provide a structure for this meta-analysis of historical events across time and cultures, then how can we presume that students will integrate their thinking at this conceptual level?

History curricula traditionally, and to this day, appear to be a compendium of events and key figures to be memorized and studied. A favored thinking skill in classrooms asks students to "Identify the causes and effects of . . ."

History standards and most history textbooks are laden with a pregnant fact base that precludes, on its face, meta-analysis, active engagement in the learning process, and a recognition of personal

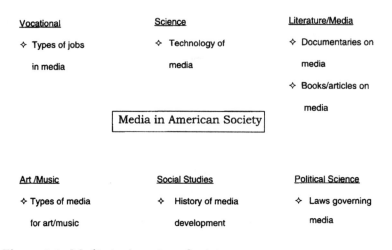

Figure 3.1. Media in American Society

relevance for students. Why is history one of the least liked subjects by students in school? Why do we continue to add content topics to a continually swelling discipline without providing a conceptual structure that will allow students (and teachers) to integrate new knowledge into their fund of information and truly begin to understand the transferable lessons of history?

Coordinated, Multidisciplinary Units Versus Integrated, Interdisciplinary Units

The majority of instructional units being designed in classrooms around the country today are what I would refer to as "coordinated, multidisciplinary" rather than "integrated, interdisciplinary." The two examples (Figures 3.1 and 3.2) compare the similarities and differences.

In the first example, teachers have chosen a specific topic, "Media in American Society, 1950-2010." As students work with this topic, they rush to the encyclopedias, Internet, and other sources to research "the fact base" related to this topic. The lack of a conceptual lens leaves this study at a lower cognitive level. Although there are a variety of disciplines participating in the unit, they are not working together in an interdisciplinary manner. The lack of a conceptual lens

Figure 3.2. Media as a Persuasive Force

to tie the focus of the disciplines together leaves them at a multidisciplinary level.

In the second example, Figure 3.2, teachers have the students view the topic through the conceptual lens of "persuasive force." The conceptual theme and focus of the unit becomes "Media as a Persuasive Force in American Society." Students can no longer just access and regurgitate researched information on the topic. They must now focus and integrate their thinking at a higher, conceptual level as they look for patterns and connections across specific, content-based examples. The study will have depth, rigor, and personal relevance, and the thinking process has a motivational driver. It will hold students' interest because the issue is relevant to their own lives, and they are developing and supporting their personal analysis of the issue.

The second example qualifies as a well-designed, integrated, interdisciplinary unit for the following reasons:

- There is a conceptual lens that forces thinking above the fact base.
- The topic becomes a tool for understanding conceptual ideas that transfer across time and cultures.
- Each discipline in the web has depth and integrity as a study on its own; it is not a little art, a little mathematics, a little history, and so forth.

It is important to note that concept-based, integrated units can be developed both within disciplines (intradisciplinary) and across disciplines (interdisciplinary). Teachers who are departmentalized, and who work in a situation that does not use block schedules or teaming, can still teach conceptually and foster integrated, conceptual thinking. The key is to assign a conceptual lens to the study of major topics in their discipline and to teach to significant transferable understandings by using the fact base as a tool.

If I am a calculus teacher doing a unit on Cartesian coordinates, then I might view the topic through the conceptual lens of a line. What transferable understandings can I teach students about the concept of line through this topic of Cartesian coordinates?

If I am a history teacher doing a unit on the U.S. Constitution, then I might use a dual conceptual lens of freedom and responsibility. What transferable understandings can I teach students about the concepts of freedom and responsibility through the topic of the U.S. Constitution? Note also that the concepts of freedom and responsibility can be exemplified at other points in this history course, such as during a consideration of the Emancipation Proclamation. As concepts spiral through a curriculum and are grounded by new yet relevant topics, the student gains increasing conceptual depth and understanding.

If I am a primary grade teacher doing a science unit on dinosaurs, then I might view the topic through the conceptual lens of extinction. What essential and transferable understandings can I teach students about the concept of extinction through this topic of dinosaurs?

We can achieve high-level integration (i.e., "integrated thinking") within disciplines and among disciplines as long as we design our units of instruction using a conceptual lens to focus thinking to the conceptual level—where knowledge transfers.

The Power of the Conceptual Lens in Integration

A conceptual lens on a topic of study creates a metacognitive study. There is a purpose for the study that goes far beyond the evaluation and memorization of information related to the topic. The conceptual lens sets a target for the study that supersedes the specific topic and the moment. The focus for teaching and learning becomes the ideas that can be taken forward and applied in new but related contexts. The topic becomes the vehicle for allowing students to apply new knowledge to past knowledge as they integrate their thinking around the bigger ideas that transfer through time and across cultures. As students integrate new examples into their conceptual schema, they gain deeper understanding of the lessons of history, the principles of mathematics, the nuances of artistic knowing, and the delicate relationships of man and nature.

There are two major reasons why curriculum design should shift from a topical focus to a conceptual focus:

1. Knowledge is expanding exponentially. We cannot just add a new history or science text each year. Students need to learn the skills of accessing multiple data sources and applying the skills of critical, creative, and integrated thinking to assimilate, sort, and pattern information.
2. In this world of rapid change and global interaction, citizens need conceptual thinking abilities to understand increasingly complex social, political, and economic relationships.

When asked why American history instruction seems to crash at the end of World War II, or in the Vietnam era, a veteran teacher hesitantly offered this perspective: "Perhaps it is because, as teachers, we are more comfortable with our training and knowledge of past history and feel less confident in dealing with the complex issues of contemporary history—except at the opinion level." So how do we build more confidence with instruction in contemporary history? Our young citizens must begin to experience the complexities of American economics and politics in the global context.

Perhaps we should consider the introduction of a course with a title such as "America in a Global Context" in the middle or high school level. We know that hammering away at a set of facts related to American history, from pre-Colombian to the post-Civil War era in the eighth grade, is a discouraging uphill battle. When students enter 11th grade, the teachers complain, "Those middle school teachers didn't teach them anything." Well, they did cover the material, but the students saw no personal relevance. Wouldn't a social studies program that increases the focus on the story of American history at Grade 7, and also in the elementary grades (such as early American history in

Grade 4 along with the study of regions, and the Revolutionary and post-Revolutionary period in Grade 5) give us some flexibility to engage students at the eighth grade with a more contemporary and engaging look at American political, social, and economic issues in the contemporary global context? A course of this nature would allow students (many of whom will not go on to postsecondary schooling) to analyze the complex relationships affecting U.S. trade, business, immigration, social demographics, and so on. Not only would this course be more interesting, but students would be forced to apply complex thinking abilities. They would also begin to experience the responsibilities associated with informed and thoughtful citizenship.

If I develop a unit on "U.S. Trade in a Global Society" for this course, I have a wide variety of conceptual lenses from which to select, but each lens will alter the focus of the unit. The choice of a conceptual lens to focus a topic of study determines a path for the thinking process. Listed below are possible concepts that could focus my unit on U.S. trade:

- Interdependence/dependence
- Conflict
- Competition
- Supply and demand
- Change

If I choose the lens of conflict for my unit, then all of the topics selected for study need to illuminate that concept in relation to the theme. The topics selected to illuminate the lens of conflict as related to "U.S. Trade in a Global Society" will differ from the topics selected for a study of change as related to "U.S. Trade in a Global Society." Realize that even if I choose the lens of change for my unit, I can still deal with conflict as a topic or subconcept within the unit. But I will be looking at conflict through the lens of change: How and why has conflict related to trade relationships changed over time? Another interesting technique would have students work in small groups investigating the same theme but using different conceptual lenses for different perspectives. One group might look at the theme of trade through the lens of interrelationships; another might view the theme through the lens of balance of power.

Teachers will not know all of the information supporting an issues-based unit of study up front. They are learners along with the students. But they do need to stay current with the facts and ideas of contemporary issues by reading and viewing multiple sources of information—books, magazines, newspapers, the Internet, television, and so on. They also need to practice the complex thinking abilities that they expect their students to learn by seeking, verifying, and analyzing information at both the concrete and conceptual levels—looking for patterns and connections, and drawing out important understandings related to facts and deeper conceptual ideas. Raising academic standards has more to do with elevating thinking processes than with covering more topics.

Unit Planning Pages

Figure 3.3 (a-d) provides three unit planning pages that can be used to lay out a concept-process teaching unit. Figure 3.3d is the secondary school format for Figure 3.3c. These pages correlate with the nine unit planning steps outlined in Figure 3.4.

The nine steps, which are described in the following section, update the unit design steps provided in my earlier book, *Stirring the Head, Heart and Soul: Redefining Curriculum and Instruction* (1995, Corwin Press). The notes that follow the nine steps provide additional information to facilitate the design process and to answer critical questions. The general model is applicable from primary grades through postsecondary schools.

Designing Integrated Units: Questions and Responses

Questions arise as teachers work together to design concept-based units. To answer some of these questions, let's take each of the nine unit design steps and discuss major issues.

1. The Unit Theme

A. *What is the difference between a "theme" and a "concept"?*

- A concept meets the following criteria: A one- or two-word mental construct that is broad and abstract, timeless, universal, and

(text continues on p. 74)

Subject Area: _____

Concept	Grade Level	Unit Theme	Essential Understandings	Essential Questions

Web:

Figure 3.3a. Unit Planning Pages

Concept: _____ Unit Theme: _____

Processes (Complex Performances)	Skills

Figure 3.3b. Unit Planning Pages

71

Weekly Plan for Unit—Elementary Level

Concept: _____ Unit Theme: _____

	Week 1	Week 2	Week 3	Week 4
Essential Understandings				
Essential Questions	Code[1]	Code[1]	Code[1]	Code[1]
Social Studies				
Science				
Visual Arts				
Music				
Literature, Media, English				
Mathematics				

Figure 3.3c. Unit Planning Pages

1. Gardner's Multiple Intelligences: Code to Activities

Weekly Plan for Unit—Secondary Levels

Concept: _____   Unit Theme: _____

	Week 1	Week 2	Week 3	Week 4
Essential Understandings				
Essential Questions				
Subject Area Activities (lecture, small group, independent, whole group, project, presentation, etc.)				

Figure 3.3d. Unit Planning Pages

1. Decide on a ***unit theme*** that will allow all team members to enter the integration process.
2. Identify a ***major concept*** to serve as a suitable ***integrating lens*** for the study.
3. Web the ***topics*** for study, by subject or area, around the concept and theme.
4. Brainstorm some of the ***essential understandings*** (***generalizations***) that you would expect students to derive from the study.
5. Brainstorm "***essential questions***" to facilitate the student's study toward the essential understandings.
6. List ***processes*** (***complex performances***) and bullet key skills to be emphisized in unit instruction and activities.
7. For each week and discipline in the unit, write ***instructional activities*** to engage students with essential questions and processes. The instructional activities and questions should help students bridge to essential understandings.
8. Write the ***culminating performance*** to show the depth of learning. The culminating performance answers the question, "What do I want students to know and be able to do as a result of this integrated unit of study?"
9. Design the ***scoring guide*** (criteria and standard) to assess the performance task. Decide on additional types of assessments to measure progress throughout the unit.

Figure 3.4. Steps for Integrated Unit Design

represents a variety of examples that all share the attributes of the concept.

- A theme can be topical, such as "Dinosaurs" or "The American Civil War"; or it can be conceptual, such as "Dinosaurs and Extinction" or "Conflict During the American Civil War." *Including the concept as part of the unit title changes a topical theme into a conceptual theme.* Which type of theme requires a greater degree of complex thinking?
- You can state your unit focus as a topical theme, but for higher-level integration, you will also want to identify a conceptual lens for the unit.

B. *How can I match the theme of my unit*
to the time frame allotted for the study?

- The theme of the unit is the centering topic, issue, problem, or question under study. You want to limit the theme of the unit to fit your time frame. Is it a 1-week unit? Three weeks? Six weeks? If I do a unit on "America," I'll be busy for a long time; but if I limit the theme to "U.S. Politics in the 20th Century" (the conceptual lens of partisanship might be fun!), I have defined a theme to fit a shorter time frame. The more words you add to the unit theme, the tighter the time frame. A unit on birds in the elementary grades could be quite lengthy, but a theme of "Migratory Birds in the Pacific Northwest" (with a conceptual lens of migration, perhaps) uses qualifiers to tighten the time frame.

C. *How do the number of disciplines*
participating in a unit affect the unit theme?

- Generally, the more subjects involved in the unit, the broader and more abstract the theme. To allow each discipline to enter the integration process, the theme has to be broad enough to encompass the different curricula. For example, I could do a unit titled "The Force of Magnets" with a conceptual lens of force, but if I want to include social studies in the same unit, then I would have to make the theme more abstract and broad, such as "Forces in Our World." As you can see, this makes the theme so obtuse that it provides little focus, and the unit will lack coherence. We end up with many disparate examples of force in science, social systems, literature, and so on. So beware the pit of "thematic obtuseness."

2. *Concept (Conceptual Lens)*

A. *Why use a conceptual lens for my topic of study?*

- A conceptual lens (focus concept) forces thinking to the integration level. Students see patterns and connections at a conceptual level as they relate the topic to the broader study framed by the lens.

- Without a conceptual lens, a topic of study remains at a lower cognitive level, and students seek to memorize the facts related to the topic.

- The focus concept facilitates and requires deep understanding, and it allows for the transfer of knowledge.

B. *How do I select a suitable conceptual lens?*

- The first step is to recognize the difference between a topic, such as "The American Civil War," which implies a specific body of facts to be learned, and a concept, such as *civil strife*, which is a broader, more abstract construct.

- The second step is to look at the theme of your unit and select a suitable conceptual lens to provide a direction for the thinking process. For example, do you want thinking to center around "Conflict During the American Civil War" or "Freedom and Justice During the American Civil War"? For beginners in concept-based unit design, it sometimes helps to refer to the concepts suggested previously in Figure 2.3, realizing that there are other choices available that are not shown on the sample lists.

C. *Shouldn't I decide on my conceptual lens*
before I decide on the theme of my unit?

- Not usually. How would you know which lens would provide the greatest thinking power unless you relate it to the specific topic you are studying? Occasionally, you can decide as a teaching team that a particular concept is so important that you want to focus the study around that concept and the lessons related to it. This usually occurs when teachers want to do a unit related to an area of human values, such as responsibility or cooperation. However, these units too often turn into what I call "Thou shalt . . . units" because the essential understandings usually ring like church bells: "If people cooperate, they have more friends" or "If you are responsible, you will succeed."

To make these value area units more effective, consider the significance of the value to society and then focus the concept around a topic of study that grounds it in this significance. For example, the theme of a unit with the conceptual lens of responsibility might be "Responsibility, Citizenship, and Strong Communities." For cooperation, the unit theme might be "The Power of Communication and Cooperation in Families." These themes call for deeper thinking and can deliver more powerful understandings.

3. Webbing the Topics for Study

A. Should the categories around the web always be different subject areas?

- No. There are two key considerations when deciding on categories to display the specific topics of study related to the theme:
  — Is the unit "interdisciplinary"? If it is, then show the different subject areas that are participating in the unit as your categories.
  — Is the unit "intradisciplinary"? If so, then you might show the different disciplines of study that appear within the subject area field as your categories. For example, if I am doing a unit within the field of social studies, my categories might be the disciplines of history, geography, economics, and government. However, an intradisciplinary study of this type should also at least be interdisciplinary enough to include literature/media and mathematics. To study any topic within the social studies or science fields without considering the related literature/media and applications of mathematics greatly shortchanges the study for students.

  If the unit is intradisciplinary, a teacher or group of teachers might choose to determine the categories that best break down the theme into its significant components. For example, world language teachers may choose to do a unit related to the concept of culture ("The Impact of Spanish Culture on the United States") and would define the categories around the web by the elements of culture: language, customs, music and art, family, occupations, and so on.

Similarities and Differences

Art
✧ Torn paper bears: **shape, size**
✧ Bear paintings: **color, texture**
✧ Masks: **symmetry, color**
✧ Bear drawings: **line, rhythm**

Science
✧ Types of bears
✧ **Habitats**
✧ **Social habits**
✧ **Needs:** Food, shelter
✧ **Lifespan-cycles**
✧ **Predators**

Music
✧ *Running Bear:* **rhythm, rhyme**
✧ *Bear Went Over the Mountain:* **melody, pitch**

Bears in the Global Village

Literature/Media
✧ Legends on bears
✧ Bear fact books (draw out concepts such as **legend, habitats,** and **habits**)

Mathematics
✧ Measurement (**size, weight**)
✧ Populations of (**more than, less than, number**)
✧ Lifespan (**graph**)

Figure 3.5. Bears in the Global Village: Concept Web

B. How do we maintain the integrity of disciplines in interdisciplinary units?

- Many secondary teachers express concern that their discipline is merely a "handmaiden" to either social studies or science, because integrated unit themes often come from these areas. The key to maintaining the integrity of different disciplines in the integration process is for each subject area to identify and teach to its own discipline-based concepts. The identification of subject area concepts is accomplished during the webbing process. Figures 3.5 and 3.6 show two examples, one elementary and one secondary, that illustrate how discipline-based concepts should be identified for each subject. Sometimes, the topic identified will actually be a general concept, such as "habitats," but at other times, the topic will be very specific, such as "ant colonies." In the case of specific topics, it is helpful to list the related concepts to the right of the topic on the web (see examples in Figures 3.5 and 3.6). Please note that even though you are teaching the concepts of each discipline, your unit remains integrated and interdisciplinary

Figure 3.6. Citizenship: Concept Web
SOURCE: Adapted from Figure 4.10, *Stirring the Head, Heart, and Soul* by H. Lynn Erickson, p. 114. Copyright © 1995, Corwin Press, Inc.

because of the focus on the common unit theme and conceptual lens.

C. *Why is discipline integrity important?*

- If we cannot maintain the integrity of disciplines (i.e., conceptual integrity), then we should not design interdisciplinary units. Disregarding the conceptual base of the different disciplines leads to the "handmaiden" phenomenon. In a handmaiden design, all of the essential understandings from the unit of study relate to the unit theme, which is usually based in the social or physical world (social studies or science). In a concept-based model, the essential understandings for each discipline show a balance—some understandings relate to the unit theme, and some understandings express the essential understandings of the specific discipline as demonstrated through the unit theme (Figures 3.7 and 3.8).

D. *How are concepts used in integrated units?*

- One, and sometimes two, concepts serve as a focus lens for a unit. The focus concept is referred to as the "conceptual lens"

Bears in a Global Village

Science: *Predators* can disrupt animal *habitats*.
Animals control their *environment* to meet their *needs*.
The *lifespan* of different *animals* varies.

Mathematics: The *size* of *objects* can be represented
with *numbers*.
Changes in animal *populations* can be graphed
over *time*.

Art: The *size* and *shape* of *objects* can be represented visually.
Primary colors can be combined to create new *colors*.

Note: Kindergarten and first grade teachers may want to
substitute the word *bears* for *animals*.

Figure 3.7. Sample Discipline-Based Generalizations for Figure 3.5

for the unit. But realize that many other subconcepts are taught as topics under each subject around the web. Concepts are used in two ways in units:

— To help students understand conceptual attributes by experiencing a concept across a myriad of examples

— To help students learn how to identify and understand major conceptual ideas (generalizations and principles) that emerge out of the study of specific topics in each discipline.

To maintain the integrity of the different disciplines, some interdisciplinary teams choose a focus concept and then let each team "do its own thing" in its curriculum as long as the content ties to the focus concept. This approach may help students understand the attributes of a concept across a variety of examples, but it does nothing to help students integrate their thinking around a common theme, problem, issue, or question by drawing on the offerings of each discipline. Without discipline coherence—all subjects focusing on the conceptual theme—there would be no interdisciplinarity. The disciplines would not be working together to reinforce each other or to facilitate deep and focused understanding of the common issue.

Conflicting Notions of Citizenship

Social Studies: *Family, religion, ethnicity,* and other group and
cultural influences contribute to the
development of *values, beliefs,* and practices.
Conflicting notions of *citizenship* can create *social*
and *political tensions.*
Social and *political tensions* reflect issues of *power*
and *control* between *groups.*

Literature/Media: *Literature* and *media* persuade *public opinion.*
Governments set varying *limits* on *free*
expression.

Mathematics: The accuracy of *growth projection* relies on the
interaction of *independent variables* over *time.*

Music: *Lyrics, rhythm,* and *tone* express *message* and *feeling.*
Music conveys the *values* and *beliefs* of a *culture* or *group.*

Figure 3.8. Sample Discipline-Based Generalizations for Figure 3.6

E. What is the role of mathematics in the integration process?

- Mathematics serves as a process tool in integrated units. Integrated units show students how mathematics is applied in real-world contexts to explain phenomena and solve problems. Mathematics resembles the language arts in integrated units. It is applied across the disciplines as a thinking and process tool. For too long, we have allowed mathematics to work in a box, isolated from the rest of the curriculum. We would never think of working with the language arts areas of reading and writing without a context, yet we have been doing so for 100 years with mathematics instruction. It is true that mathematics must have a time for direct skill instruction. But the application of those skills flows naturally into integrated units of study. Where else can we find a context that brings so many different disciplines together to investigate an important problem, topic, or issue? Mathematics teachers should be overjoyed to have an opportunity to show how important mathematics is to the other disciplines. What a forum for demonstrating the power of mathematics in our everyday lives!

F. How do I identify the topics for the
mathematics category on the web?

- Mathematics is the last subject to be webbed. After all of the other disciplines have defined their topics for study, take mathematics out of the box and ask the question, "How can mathematics be applied to extend understanding of the topics listed under history, economics, geography, music, art, media, science, and so on?" Brainstorm all of the possible applications of mathematics related to the different subject area topics. Do not list mathematics activities on the web (e.g., "Estimate the dimensions of colonial ships"); just identify the mathematics processes and concepts at this time (estimation, percentage, etc.). The determination of specific activities comes later in the planning process.

G. Does interdisciplinary integration require
that all subjects be included in the study?

- No. The key to higher-level integration is the conceptual lens that takes thinking beyond the study of facts related to a topic. You should bring only those disciplines into the study that deepen understanding of the unit theme in relation to the conceptual lens. Following are two considerations as to how subjects and their topics of study should be selected to complete the webbing:
  — You should not force both social studies and science into every unit. Although the conceptual lens can be treated by topics in both disciplines, the content may be so disparate that students would experience cognitive dissonance. I would not want to deal with cycles of human history in the same unit that I am dealing with cycles in the animal world. This unit would lack coherence and could not be considered interdisciplinary even though the conceptual lens of cycles is shared in common. This topic dissonance is a common error in unit development today.

On the flip side, however, science and social studies do fit well together in some units. If the theme has both physical world and social world implications, then science and social studies can share a sedan; otherwise, they should take their own cars. Environmental issues or technology and society themes work well with the duality of subjects.

— When you are deciding on topics for each of the discipline categories, ask the question: "Which topics would best develop understanding of this theme with this conceptual lens?" Remember that different conceptual lenses affect the choice of topics under the discipline headings.

4. Generalizations (Essential Understandings)

A. What are "generalizations"?

- Generalizations fall on the synthesis level of thinking in Figure 1.1. They may be referred to as essential understandings because they are the deeper, transferable ideas that arise from fact-based studies.
- Generalizations are statements of conceptual relationship.
- Generalizations transfer through time and across cultures. They are exemplified through the fact base but transcend singular examples.
- Generalizations have characteristics similar to "concept":
  — Broad and abstract
  — Generally timeless (the truth of generalizations have to be continually tested)
  — Universal
  — Examples vary across situations but support the truth of the generalization

B. How do we identify generalizations for our topics of study?

- In units of study, use the content web to look for concepts that can be paired to make statements of essential understanding. Why are you studying the topic? What do you want students to understand at a conceptual, transferable level—beyond the specific topic?

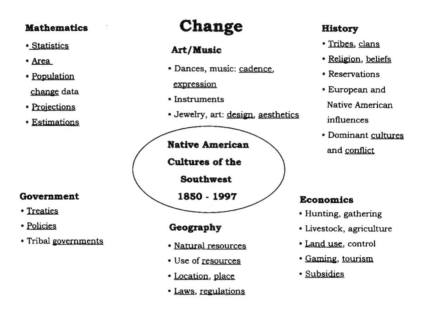

Mathematics
- Statistics
- Area
- Population change data
- Projections
- Estimations

Change

Art/Music
- Dances, music: cadence, expression
- Instruments
- Jewelry, art: design, aesthetics

Native American Cultures of the Southwest 1850 - 1997

History
- Tribes, clans
- Religion, beliefs
- Reservations
- European and Native American influences
- Dominant cultures and conflict

Government
- Treaties
- Policies
- Tribal governments

Geography
- Natural resources
- Use of resources
- Location, place
- Laws, regulations

Economics
- Hunting, gathering
- Livestock, agriculture
- Land use, control
- Gaming, tourism
- Subsidies

Figure 3.9. Native American Cultures Web

Let's try an example. If you were to teach a unit related to the theme "Native American Cultures of the Southwest," you might teach the topics shown in Figure 3.9.

Notice the underlined concepts around the web (e.g., treaties, religion, population change). Now look at the different concepts and ask yourself the question, "What do I really want students to understand about "Treaties" or "Land Use," or "Religion and Beliefs"? Pair different concepts to create generalizations—important understandings that go beyond the facts but are supported by the facts.

C. How do we write generalizations?

- When first learning, it is helpful to use the sentence starter, "Students understand that . . ." Complete the sentence by pairing two or more concepts from your unit of study into a sentence conveying an important idea that will transfer through time and across cultures.

- When writing generalizations, do not mention your topic of study. In other words, do not use proper or personal nouns. Move beyond the example provided by your topic and look for the transcending ideas. For example, in my unit on Native Americans, I would not just teach the fact that "Native Americans of the Southwest express their cultural beliefs and values through art"; I would generalize to the idea that has greater transfer value: "Cultures express beliefs and values through art." The example of Native Americans would be my teaching tool. When students begin to relate specific examples to the broader idea, they systematically build conceptual depth and understanding over time as they meet new examples. We cannot assume that students will make this transfer intuitively.

- When writing generalizations, use active, present-tense verbs to convey the timeless characteristic. Avoid passive voice and past-tense verbs. Try to avoid the use of "to be" verbs (is, are, have). A pitfall in writing generalizations, which are statements of conceptual relationship, is to write them as simple definitions of concepts. An example might be the statement, "Scale is a range of possible values for a measured property." This statement has several concepts (underlined), but it is mainly a definition of the concept of scale. The use of a "to be" verb is often a clue that a definition has been offered. The danger is in overusing definitions and missing the conceptual ideas that frame the deeper knowledge of the study.

- Use qualifiers (may, can, often) if your generalization may not hold across all examples, but is still significant as an understanding.

  Let's put two or more of the following concepts together and state a generalization. (You can get at least five generalizations out of these concepts.) You may use other concepts if you need to add to the list for your idea.

Migration	Change	Culture
Interdependence	Conflict	Perspectives

Is your idea important for students to understand in a broader context? Did you remember to use an active, present-tense verb? Do you have a full sentence? Did you avoid using proper and personal nouns? Did you use a qualifier if the generalization is important but may not hold across all examples? (e.g., "Migration may lead to cultural conflicts").

D. What is the difference between a generalization and a principle?

- Generalizations are statements of conceptual relationship that transfer across examples. They must be continually tested for truth because they may not hold over time. Some generalizations meet the test of timelessness, but they may not be ideas that hold as much significance as principles in the structure of a discipline.

  Principles are always true and have significant roles in a discipline. They are the cornerstones for understanding and applying the knowledge of a discipline. They carry the weight of universal and timeless truth, such as Newton's laws of gravity or the axioms of mathematics.

E. How do we tell the difference between "less sophisticated" and "more sophisticated" generalizations?

- If we think of generalizations according to "levels" of sophistication, then we can look at what characteristics differentiate Level 1 (less sophisticated) to Level 3 (sophisticated) generalizations. The following generalizations, which might be appropriate for the primary grades, show three different levels of sophistication.

  Level 1: *People* of different *cultures* show *similarities and differences.*

  Level 2: *Culture* influences the *dress, customs,* and *behavior* of a *people.*

  Level 3: *Cultural diversity* can lead to *conflict.*

  As we move forward from Level 1, the generalizations become more specific and the concept load becomes heavier. The concepts (in italics) require more background knowledge to understand as the levels increase. As the levels progress, we won't necessarily find more concepts in the sentence, but the idea presented will be more cognitively challenging.

  Let's look at a set of generalizations that would be more developmentally appropriate at the high school level:

Level 1: Ease of *transportation* and *communication* facilitate *global interaction.*

Level 2: Increases in *global interaction* lead to increasing *complexity* in *economic, political,* and *social systems.*

Level 3: As the *social, economic,* and *political systems* of a *society* increase in *complexity,* issues of *power* and *control* create *conflict* and lead to greater individual *identification* with specific *group ideologies* or views.

F. How do we "scaffold" thinking in order to write generalizations at more sophisticated levels?

- To take thinking to more sophisticated levels in writing generalizations, it is helpful to use open-ended, essential questions, just as you would do in the teaching situation. Notice the essential questions following each generalization in the examples below. The questions are formed by asking a "how" or "why" (not a "what") question related to the generalization. In the unit planning process, teachers discuss the possible answers to the essential question and listen for any concepts that could be used to form a more sophisticated essential understanding (generalization). Make certain that the generalizations answer the essential question and avoid the error of restating the previous generalization in different words.

  Notice that the generalizations become more concept-specific as the levels increase, but the concepts require greater background knowledge.

  Elementary schools:

  Level 1: "All *cultures* have *celebrations.*"
  — Why do cultures have celebrations?

  Level 2: "*Celebrations* express the *traditions* of a *culture.*"
  — Why are traditions important to a culture?

  Level 3: "*Traditions* reflect the *beliefs, values,* and *heritage* of a *culture.*"

  Secondary schools:

  Level 1: "*Organisms* survive in *diverse environments.*"
  — How do organisms survive?

Level 2: *"Biological adaptations* change *structures, behaviors,* or *physiology* and enhance *reproductive success.*

— How do organisms change behaviors?

Level 3: "An organism's *behavioral responses* to *stimuli* evolve through *natural selection* (and often exhibit an *evolutionary logic*).

Note that the parenthetical addition in Level 3 creates a Level 4 generalization.

Take the Level 1 generalization provided below and scaffold by asking a "how" or "why" question that will take the thinking to the next level. Notice that the Level 1 generalization in this example, and in some of the previous examples, uses a "to be" verb. This occurs most often at Level 1 because the idea is a simple and quite obvious statement of conceptual fact. As the generalizations become more sophisticated, other verbs usually carry more power for the idea expressed. Using "is," "are," or "have" at Level 1 is acceptable, although not preferred.

Level 1 generalization: "Governments limit the freedoms of citizens."

    Essential question: _____?

Level 2 generalization: _____

    Essential question: _____?

Level 3 generalization: _____

Did you experience difficulty moving from Level 2 to Level 3? This is common. I think it is because our traditional curricular design does not require much thinking beyond Level 1 or Level 2. So here is a tip to help you reach Level 3. After you have written the Level 2 generalization, ask the significance question, "So what? What importance or significance does this understanding (generalization) have for society, the individual, and so on?" After thinking about and discussing the significance, write the importance in the form of a Level 3 generalization.

G. *Aren't generalizations too abstract to mean very much?*
Isn't it more important to have clarity and topic specificity?

- The most specific and clear piece of information is a fact (see following example), but is it the desired end for teaching and learning? What do you think? Why? What role do facts play in concept/process curriculum and instruction?
  - — *Fact:* U.S. industries are opening factories in foreign countries.
  - — *Generalization:* <u>Global competition</u> in business requires <u>economic strategies</u> to lower <u>costs</u> and increase <u>production</u>.

  Note that concepts are underlined in the generalization.

  Do not underestimate the power of a seemingly bland generalization. The questions that are generated from the generalization challenge thinking and take discussions to deeper levels. The generalizations are the summary of higher-level thought. They bring closure to study.

H. *Why should we scaffold generalizations?*

- When teachers are asked why they are teaching a topic, the first answer is usually a summary of the facts they want students to know. After learning how to identify and write generalizations, teachers begin to state the important transferable ideas they want students to understand. But this new skill takes practice. The first generalizations are more often Level 1, no matter what the grade level. The learning curve is very steep, however, and after a few practice sessions, the generalizations become more sophisticated. Learning how to scaffold thinking also helps the thinking and writing processes. Learning to use language precisely to state essential understandings brings focus to teaching and learning. The verbs *influence, affect,* or *to be* often indicate a Level 1 generalization because the statements that use them tend to be so general that they say very little.

  It is important to scaffold those generalizations that are so simplistic that they beg to be carried forward. You have students in your classrooms who fall at all levels of conceptual sophistication. If you identify and teach to all three levels of generalizations, you will be able to differentiate curriculum and instruction for the different ability levels while still centering around the same topics. This helps in this age of inclusionary programming.

I. Why should I determine so many of the generalizations for a unit? Why not let the students come up with their own generalizations?

- If a student comes up with a generalization in the group discussion, then celebrate! You have a thinking student! But if you are just beginning to work with a concept-based curriculum, the more likely scenario will be students who think to the level of facts (we have trained them well) and who resist thinking beyond the facts. (Do some of your brightest students come to mind?)

  The reason that teachers identify most of the unit generalizations is that we are learning how to think conceptually ourselves and need the practice; more important, we are "systematically" teaching students how to think. This is ultimately an inductive teaching model using essential questions and activities to direct thinking toward essential understandings. To teach students how to think conceptually, we have to know where the thinking is going (at least a direction) so that we can plan a questioning path. Certainly, we do not want to be so rigid that we miss "teachable moments," when a student discovers a big idea on which we can build, or when student questions take the discussion in a certain direction. But we cannot always wait and see where students want to go if we want to teach conceptual thinking and illuminate essential understandings for a unit of study.

5. Essential Questions

A. What are essential questions?

- Essential questions are a critical driver for teaching and learning. They engage students in the study and create a bridge between performance-based activities and deeper, conceptual understandings.

  Heidi Hayes-Jacobs (1997), in *Mapping the Big Picture*, states, "The essential question is conceptual commitment. In a sense

---

**Geographic Regions and Cultures
of the Pacific Northwest: Objectives**

- Understand the impact of geographic regions on the development of culture.
- Identify the geographic regions.
- Compare the regions of Washington State.
- List the geographic features for each region.
- Describe how people use their land to meet basic needs.
- Identify your enthusiasm for this study.

Figure 3.10. Sample Grade 4 Objectives

you are saying, 'This is our focus for learning. I will put my teaching skills into helping my students examine the key concept implicit in the essential question'" (pp. 26-27).

*B. Why are essential questions important
in the teaching/learning process?*

- There are a number of reasons why essential questions are important:
  — We can help students discover patterns and build personal meaning through the effective use of questions.
  — Essential questions allow for inductive teaching—guiding students to discover meaning rather than relying mainly on deductive lecture methods.
  — Essential questions are one of the most powerful tools for helping students think at more complex levels.
- Essential questions have far greater power in the instructional process than do our traditional "objectives." I agree with Hayes-Jacobs (1997) that "when the curriculum is formed around questions [rather than objectives,] the clear message to the students is that you are probing with them" (p. 26).

  Read the objectives in Figure 3.10. (I used a little writer's license on the last objective.) Do these objectives have a familiar ring? They should, because most of us were weaned and raised on them. Now move on to Figure 3.11 and read essential questions related to the same topic.

**Geographic Regions and Cultures
of the Pacific Northwest: Essential Questions**

- Why do regions differ?
- How do regions in the Pacific Northwest differ?
- Why do different cultures use land differently?
- How do the arts of Native American cultures reflect their natural surroundings?
- Why do Native American arts so often reflect nature?
- How is a culture affected by its geography?
- How is geography affected by a culture?

Figure 3.11. Sample Grade 4 Essential Questions

What did you notice as you read the questions, and how did that differ from reading the objectives? Did you find that your mind was on autopilot as you read the objectives, but that you were *thinking* as you read the questions? Did the questions engage your interest because you wanted to know how you would personally answer them based on your own knowledge and perspectives? Why do so many curriculum documents attempt to drive content teaching through the use of objectives when they create so little passion for thinking and learning? Could it be that objectives are easier to test and score? Do we really need content objectives if we have identified clearly the critical content topics (without verbs) that students are to study, the essential understandings (generalizations) to be drawn from content, and the key processes (complex performances) and skills? We will consider the issue of objectives once again in Chapter 5 as they are related to national, state, and district standards.

C. *Why are essential questions so difficult to write?*

- We can pull only so many questions out of the air that are related to a topic. Consequently, most of the questions end up being "what" questions directly related to the topic of study. However, emphasizing "what" questions won't guide thinking to deeper waters.

One reason that teachers are having trouble writing essential questions is that they have not consciously identified the conceptual ideas (generalizations) toward which the questions should be focused. Consequently, the questions keep flowing toward the specific topic. Remember, in a concept-based curriculum, it is not enough to teach only the facts related to a specific topic; we want to use questions to take thinking to the level of conceptual understanding and help students build a schema for knowledge transfer. We need "why" and "how" questions to extend thinking.

D. How do you write essential questions?

- Writing quality essential questions for instructional units can be challenging. The following technique should help. After you have written generalizations for your unit as discussed earlier, turn the generalizations into questions as a first step. For example, if I have a generalization in Grade 2 social studies that states, "Community members have roles," then I might ask, "Why do community members have roles? If I have a generalization in mathematics and science that states, "The mass of any object increases with its velocity," then I would ask, "Why does the mass of any object increase with its velocity?" Answering the question leads to a more sophisticated generalization, "Velocity generates energy, which converts to mass."

  Lake Washington School District in Redmond, Washington is developing a quality set of essential questions that takes thinking to the conceptual level. Read the social studies excerpt from Lake Washington in Figure 3.12 and determine what quality in the questions challenges the conceptual level of thinking. Can you find some generalizations embedded in their questions?

  One reason that essential questions are difficult to write is that they need to focus not only on fact-based information but also on ideas that flow from the fact base. If teachers have not consciously identified the ideas beyond the facts in their unit planning, then the essential questions are difficult to write. We are well trained in writing questions directed to specific facts. These questions often begin with "what." It is the "how" and

---

Individuality and Interdependence: Essential Questions

- How do nations promote self-preservation (e.g., defense, resources, national organizations)?
- How do changes within nations influence interactions among them?
- How are individual rights valued and promoted in a democratic society?
- How do the values of a culture influence the roles and rights of the individual?
- How can individual rights and a government's view of the common good create stability or conflict?
- How does individual initiative impact a society?
- How does anticipating and planning for needed societal change empower individuals and groups in a democratic society?

Figure 3.12. Social Studies Essential Questions, Excerpt—Level 4, Grades 9 and 10
SOURCE: Lake Washington School District, Redmond, Washington. Copyright © 1997. Used by permission.

"why" questions that require the teacher's conceptual understanding prior to instruction.

Although factually based questions are important to ensure the foundations of knowledge, it is the open-ended, conceptually based questions that challenge the thinking of students beyond the facts. Open-ended questions that contain two or more concepts usually specify the essential understanding as an embedded statement. The Lake Washington School District, highlighted in Chapter 1, wrote very broad essential understandings. The power of their curriculum lies in the open-ended, conceptually based essential questions. It is the use of these questions as a follow-up to specific, topic-related questions that will help students bridge to deeper understanding.

Essential questions, both specific and open-ended, are used to engage students with activities that develop processes and skills and lead to content knowledge and conceptual understanding.

6. *Processes and Skills*

A. What is the difference between a process and a skill?

- A *process* can be thought of as a "complex performance." When we think of professionals doing their work, they are carrying out complex performances that require a range of abilities and knowledge.

  Skills are the specific abilities that must be learned in order to carry out the broader complex performance. In other words, skills nest in process.

B. Why do we need to identify key processes and skills for each discipline?

- If you review the national standards, you will see that processes and skills are clearly specified, because it is impossible to be a mathematician, scientist, or social scientist if you have not learned the discipline-based ways of doing and thinking.

C. Can't we just put generic language arts skills into our curriculum frameworks and then apply them across different disciplines?

- This is basically what we have done in the traditional designs of the past. But there have been two problems. Discipline-based teachers at the secondary level often viewed processes and skills as the work of the language arts teacher and not their domain. They saw their work as the content and particular skills of their discipline. Second, if we are to develop the different ways of knowing and doing across the disciplines, then we need to identify the processes and component skills that the professionals use in their work. If we can teach children to think and perform like scientists, artists, and so on, then we are giving them valuable process abilities to apply in a multidimensional world. Figure 3.13 provides an example of how a process and related skills might look on the unit planning pages.

  Notice that we are not writing activities yet. We are just identifying the complex performances (processes) and key skills that will be taught directly by the teacher. The activities,

Concept: _____	Unit Theme: _____	
Processes (Complex Performances)	*Skills*
Science: • Design and conduct a scientific investigation.	**Science:** • Formulate questions. • Conduct systematic observations. • Make accurate measurements. • Identify and control variables. • Interpret data; clarify ideas. • Generate explanations from evidence. • Propose alternative explanations. • Critique explanations and procedures.

Figure 3.13. Processes and Skills: Science

drawing on the identified processes and skills, are developed
on the next page of the unit plans.

7. *Instructional Activities*

A. *What is the purpose of the instructional activities?*

- Instructional activities are where "know" and "do" join
  hands. We design activities (as well as provide students with
  choice) so that students will have opportunities to practice
  complex performances and key skills, and so they will be able
  to develop and demonstrate increasing knowledge of critical,
  fact-based material and essential understandings (generalizations) that transcend the facts.

B. *Why does the unit planning page show
a place for essential understandings and
essential questions along with instructional activities?*

- To ensure that activities are integrated into units with a coherent tie to the development of knowledge and understanding,
  the planning page asks that teachers pull, from the first page
  of the unit plans, the essential understandings toward which
  they are teaching for each week in the unit. Then, teachers
  should correlate the appropriate essential questions to engage the mind. The next step asks, "What activities can be
  used to engage students with these essential questions that
  will lead to the essential understandings?" In other words,
  there should be a coherent link between the activities, the
  questions, and the understandings.

  When deciding on activities, look back at the processes and
  skills identified on the second planning page and make certain that you are incorporating them either as a direct instruction lesson or as a practice.

C. *How do the secondary school unit
planning pages differ from the elementary pages?*

- The secondary school remains quite departmentalized across the
  country, although many have moved to interdisciplinary teams
  and block schedules. With the reality of departmentalization,

the unit planning pages are used somewhat differently at the secondary level. Although the interdisciplinary team works together to develop the unit theme, conceptual lens, and web, the other unit components, up to the culminating performance, can be completed independently by discipline. This is because secondary teachers in a departmentalized situation will be teaching their own discipline within their own classroom. They will still be providing integrated instruction with their team because they share a common theme and conceptual lens. There will be a few major generalizations that all disciplines support, but it is critical that each discipline maintain instructional integrity by also teaching to its own generalizations that have been reached through discipline-driven questions and activities. The activities will draw on the processes and skills important to each discipline. Once the unit planning pages have been completed by each discipline, it is important that the interdisciplinary team come back together once again to share its work and discuss what the overall student learning experience will be throughout the unit. Teachers will want to maintain a holistic sense of the integrated learning experience for students.

8. Culminating Performance

A. *What is the culminating performance?*

- The culminating performance allows you to make a final assessment on how well students relate content to transferable, conceptual ideas, and on how well they are able to perform with their knowledge. It answers the question, "What do I want students to know, understand, and be able to do as a result of this unit of study?" We are assessing understanding of one or more major ideas (generalizations) for the unit, supported by critical content knowledge and demonstrated through a complex performance.

B. *How do we evaluate the culminating performance?*

- A scoring guide is developed as part of the unit planning process to assess the level of performance. It is important to

• *WHAT*	Analyze, evaluate, investigate ...
• *WHY*	in order to ...
• *HOW*	Demonstrate understanding by ...

Figure 3.14. Culminating Performance

realize that students could easily get overloaded with major projects due in all classes at the same time in integrated units. This problem can be eased if teachers plan a common performance (e.g., a play) that would draw from the different disciplines, or if they work together to stagger the due dates. Another option would be a unit portfolio, developed throughout the length of a unit, that would include the work of the different disciplines. The assessment criteria might differ by discipline.

C. Is the culminating performance
the only assessment in the unit?

- Definitely not. Throughout a unit, you will use an array of assessments that match the kinds of learning that students are to demonstrate. Interviews, true/false assessments, multiple choice, writing tasks, oral presentations, and projects are just a few examples of assessments that provide information about different kinds of learning.

D. How do we write the culminating performance?

- A major problem with many performances being written today is that there is often little or no display of deep understanding. I think that this is once again because our traditional curriculum design only takes us to the superficial level of topics and facts. How, then, can we write assessments for deep understanding? Figure 3.14 shows a simple formula for writing a demonstration of culminating performance. This format helps to ensure an assessment of deep understanding.

Complete the formula in Figure 3.14 as follows:

What do you want students to do?

WHAT: Begin this statement with a higher-level cognitive verb, such as analyze, evaluate, or investigate, and tie it directly to the theme of your unit. The theme of the unit in the example following is "The Development of U.S. Transportation: 1920 to 2010."

Example: Analyze the development of U.S. transportation (or flight) from 1920 to 2010.

WHY: in order to . . . Complete this statement by thinking beyond the topic to the importance or significance of the study. What is the transferable lesson to be taken from this particular study?

Example: . . . in order to understand how technology advances human innovation and invention (the transferable lesson–key generalization).

HOW: Begin a new sentence that frames how you want students to demonstrate their understanding of the "why" statement. This is the critical step. If you want to measure deep understanding, then this "how" statement needs to demonstrate the "why"—not just knowledge of the facts learned in the "what" statement.

Example: You are a struggling inventor with a new product design that is an adaptation of a current innovation. The state Senate Finance Committee is hearing presentations on grant applications for technology-based inventions. It is your turn to address the committee. Deliver a clear and energetic multimedia presentation showing how technological changes and advancements shaped the historical development of your product. Present your product design as the next historical development to meet society's needs, and detail your technological adaptations and user benefits. Summarize your presentation with a sincere and reasoned request for financial support.

Notice that the performance, the "how" statement, demonstrates understanding of the "why" statement. Note also that the performance in this case is not tied directly to students' knowledge of the development of transportation, which was the particular focus of the unit study, but requires that students transfer what was learned about the relationship of technology to the advances in transportation, to technology's impact on the development of another product. This takes the performance beyond a simple regurgitation of facts related to transportation. Teachers may choose to stick with demonstrating the relationship of technology to transportation in the final performance, but they will have to think through the performance to ensure that students are asked to go beyond the facts.

What are the complex performances required in this task? Can you underline them? What kinds of criteria will I check for in the scoring guide related to the multimedia presentation (clarity of presentation, organization, enthusiasm, depth and breadth of knowledge, etc.)?

Write a culminating performance that links the "how" (presentation, project, etc.) directly to the deep understanding specified in the "why" statement.

WHAT: (analyze, evaluate, investigate) _____

_____

WHY: in order to . . . _____

_____

HOW: Demonstrate understanding by . . . _____

_____

Check back over the directions to make certain the performance reached deep understanding.

Here is one more example of a strong culminating performance:

WHAT: As one of a team of cultural anthropologists, analyze the interactions of early white settlers and Native Americans

WHY: . . . in order to realize how merging cultures influence each other.

HOW: Demonstrate understanding by focusing on and researching one aspect of early Native American and white cultures (e.g., history, arts, religion, government, daily living, land use, etc.). Drawing from your research and knowledge of contemporary culture, write a case study

---

**Scoring Guide Development
for Culminating Performance**

1. State the *mode* and *criteria* to be assessed.
2. Expand the criteria with *descriptors* to specify the detail to be assessed.
3. Determine the *format* for presenting the qualitative scale.
4. Set the *standard* for quality performance.
5. Define the levels of performance by qualifying the descriptors for each level of the rubric.

Figure 3.15. Scoring Guide Development Steps

describing the obvious impacts or influences that these merging cultures have had on each other over time. As one member of the anthropological team, present an insightful and powerful speech to the state historical society, using visuals or multimedia, detailing the positive and negative lessons to be learned from the historical study of merging cultures. (Does the *HOW* demonstrate deep understanding of the *WHY* in this task?)

9. Scoring Guide for Culminating Performance

A. What is a scoring guide?

- A scoring guide (rubric) assesses performance on a task according to defined criteria and a scaled set of performance indicators. A scoring guide assesses student progress toward the standard.

B. What are the steps for developing a scoring guide?

- The five steps are listed in Figure 3.15.

  A Scoring Guide Planner (Chart 3.1) is a helpful tool for laying out the modes, criteria, and descriptors that will be used to complete a scoring guide.

  Scoring guides can take a variety of formats. Chart 3.2 and Figure 3.16 provide two examples for assessing a culminating performance.

Mode	Criteria	Descriptors
Writing	Mechanics	Capitalization Punctuation Spelling
	Organization	Paragraphs Sequencing Topic sentence Details Transitions
	Knowledge	Accurate Relevant Depth/breadth
Project	Knowledge	Accurate Significant Thorough
Neatness	Quality	
		Style

Chart 3.1. Scoring Guide Planner

Perhaps the most difficult part of writing scoring guides is finding effective and precise language to describe performance at the various levels. Too often, the defining language sounds "wishy-washy," such as "always," "often," "sometimes," or "seldom." We need to keep working on this language problem. We can find descriptive terms that are more precise and helpful to students, but it means that teachers will need to help students develop a mental construct for what these terms "look like" in the performance or product. Figure 3.17 provides an example of more precise descriptors for two levels of performance.

Students need to see specific exemplars, representative examples, of work. They need practice in applying the various descriptors that will be used in the assessment of their own work. This process of internalizing the "look" of various levels of performance through the descriptors must be engaged prior to the student's own work on a culminating performance. It is helpful if

(text continues on p. 106)

Mode: Oral Presentation
Scoring Guide:

Criteria	Excellent	Highly Competent	Competent	Novice
Development of Ideas	More than four lifeskills developed in the story with reasonable and well-developed examples of each. Thoughtful and accurate explanation of the impact of lifeskills on learning. Engaging and effective beginning, middle, and end.	Four lifeskills developed in the story with examples of each. Detailed explanation of the impact of lifeskills on learning. Effective beginning, middle, and end to the story.	Four lifeskills mentioned in the story with examples of each. Impact of the lifeskills on learning mentioned. Story includes a beginning, middle, and end.	Fewer than four life-skills in the story with some examples included. Impact of lifeskills on learning incomplete. Evidence of a beginning and end to the story.
Delivery	Speech is well articulated with excellent volume. Movement and actions are used throughout to enhance the performance. Dialogue is delivered with exceptionally felt expression.	Speech is clear with appropriate volume. Movement and actions are used throughout the performance. Dialogue is delivered with expression.	Voice is clear with adequate volume. Movement and actions used occasionally during the performance. Dialogue is delivered with sporadic shows of feeling.	Voice is generally clear, with some changes in volume. Movement and/or actions are used little during the performance. Dialogue is delivered with a minor show of feeling.

Chart 3.2. Scoring Guide Excerpt From the "Building Community" Unit, Grade 4

SOURCE: Davenport Community Schools, Davenport, Iowa: Deb Kretschmer, Wanda Leonard. Used by permission.

Culminating Performance: As an investigative reporter, analyze the continuing problems with race relations in American society in order to illuminate and address underlying issues. Write a clear and insightful report for American readers highlighting key issues and multiple perspectives. Suggest a reasoned course of action for proactively addressing underlying issues.

Criteria:		
Content Validity	4	Precise and accurate detailing of significant race-related interactions and issues
	3	Accurate detailing of significant race-related interactions and issues
	2	Generally accurate detailing of significant race-related interactions/ issues
	1	Several publicized events described but lack accuracy in key details
Insight	4	Comprehensive and thoughtful presentation of patterns and connections between significant racial interactions and events and underlying issues. Typically presents logical and reasonable course of action based on independent analysis and a consideration of multiple perspectives
	3	Thoughtful presentation of connections between publicized racial interactions and events, and media analyses of underlying issues. Reasonable course of action typically proposed based on a personal interpretation of media analyses and publicized perspectives
	2	Presentation of a few publicized racial interactions with limited evidence linking events and underlying issues. Proposed course of action often based on personal opinion with limited attention to multiple perspectives.
	1	Presentation of one or two publicized racial interactions with generally stereotypical assumptions as to underlying cause. Course of action fails to address a relevant cause; no insight.
Writing Clarity	4	Order, structure, and presentation of information purposefully crafted to guide the reader's comprehension
	3	Order, structure, and presentation of information accurate and coherent
	2	Order, structure, and presentation of information shows direction but lacks coherence and sense of purpose
	1	Order, structure, and presentation of information fragmented but presents some information
Impact	4	Generates a deep, reflective response in the reader
	3	Generates thoughtful reflection on the part of the reader
	2	Engages reader's interest and reflection sporadically
	1	Fails to engage reader's interest or reflection

Performance Level

4 - Expert
3 - Proficient
2 - Beginner
1 - Novice

Criteria Standard = 3
Total Standard =12

Total Performance Score:

Total Performance Level

Expert
Proficient
Beginner
Novice

Figure 3.16. Sample Scoring Guide

Excellent		Highly Competent	
Excellent	Sensitive	Evident	Reasonable
Perceptive	Rational	Well-marked	Fluent
Distinct	Meticulous	Clear	Refined
Thoughtful	Conscientious	Conspicuous	Informed
Insightful	Rigorous	Marked	Bold
Clear	Precise	Well-defined	Careful
Vivid	Exceptional	Expressive	Particular
Graphic	Superior	Effective	Detailed
Striking	Cogent	Descriptive	Objective
Explicit	Noteworthy	Emphatic	Authentic
Articulate	Distinguished	Vigorous	Feasible
Notable	Original	Efficient	Balanced
Engaging	Exact	Aware	Proportioned

Figure 3.17. Scoring Guide Qualifiers

— The teacher uses the descriptors throughout the year on a variety of different performance assessments

— Teachers on a grade level agree to a common language of descriptors and applications to the various levels of performance

— Students can participate in choosing and defining the various descriptors of performance

Summary

A content-based, integrated curriculum requires a conceptual lens to draw thinking above the disciplines. The goal of an integrated curriculum should be "integrated thinking"—seeing the patterns and connections of knowledge at a conceptual and transferable level of understanding. Topics and facts are critical tools in the development of integrated thinking.

Units organized around a topical theme, without a conceptual focus, reflect "coordinated, multidisciplinary" rather than "integrated, interdisciplinary" design models. In a coordinated, multidisciplinary model, facts and activities are coordinated to a specific topic of study but lack a conceptual lens to force thinking to the level of conceptual integration. The lack of a conceptual focus also leaves the disciplines operating in a multidisciplinary, independent fashion. They more or less "do their own thing" rather than work together (interdisciplinarily) to develop the conceptual theme.

This chapter provides a basic model for designing concept-process integrated units for both interdisciplinary and intradisciplinary approaches. To assist curriculum writers, each step in the unit design process is explained.

Another area of focus and concern in education today is school-to-work integration. Chapter 4 looks at the problems and issues related to bridging the barriers between academic and occupational curriculum areas. A concept-based integration model shows how to raise the standards for both areas while maintaining field integrity.

4

Integrating Curricula in
School-to-Work Designs

Conventional Models of Curriculum Design

Teaching can be quite isolated from the rapid changes in the business world. Because a key component of education is to prepare students for success in work, it is important to understand how the world of work is structured and functioning today. What are the work skills expected of graduating students? What kind of world will they be entering as they move into a global labor market? The business world is changing dramatically and rapidly. Teachers study this phenomenon and adapt their curriculum and instruction to balance this component in the educational program with the other aspects of a well-rounded educational plan. Our educational program does not revolve solely around meeting work requirements and skill needs; but to promote the continuing economic health of our society, it is certainly one of the important components in curriculum design.

Past and present conventional models of academic curricula in the United States generally organize content by topics. Teachers feel pressured by expanding textbooks and a public that too often equates

AUTHOR'S NOTE: The material in this chapter was originally written for and first appeared in the 1996 Arizona School to Work System, Arizona State University. Reprinted with permission.

Competency 5.0. Gas Metal Arc Weld

Skill Competencies

5.1 Identify joint design.
5.2 Select and install appropriate wire size and type and correct tip.
5.3 Determine weld position.
5.4 Install and adjust flow meter.
5.5 Adjust wire feed speed, amperage, and voltage.
5.6 Make weld.

Figure 4.1. Arc Weld Competency and Skills

fund of information with intelligence. Students cover facts about rainforests, the Constitution, whales, bears, and tadpoles, but the job of teaching and learning takes on a frenetic face as fractured bits of information flash by. Accelerating change, in an interdependent and complex world, generates microchip overload. The futile attempt to teach more, at a faster pace, can result in a sterile curriculum where deep understanding is sacrificed, patterns and connections are missed, and "coverage" takes precedence over questions, experiences, and thoughtful application.

Additionally, past and present industrial models of occupational curricula in the United States too often focus on the development of discrete skills related to specific occupations, rather than on integrated skill clusters performed and transferred across complex tasks. In the industrial model, "to be or not to be"—a welder, an auto mechanic, or a secretary—depends on the ability to perform discrete skills to competency. For example, in a welding course, student competencies might be listed as shown in Figure 4.1.

The focus of curriculum and instruction in this model is skill driven. Problem solving may play a limited role, but the notions of intellectual rigor and "quality of performance" related to a broadened set of task competencies remain interesting but elusive. Certainly, students must learn these discrete skills, but the end focus for learning, in these specific competency models, is imitation rather than skill application in a broader contextualized performance. We can compare the skill development in welding to the skill development in mathematics or the language arts. Although it is important to learn the discrete skills, they broaden when contextualized in a complex, real-world performance.

To contextualize welding, a scenario might require the student to apply his or her acquired knowledge and skill from welding, science, and language arts, perhaps, to solve a problem requiring a certain kind of weld based on knowledge of science principles related to heat and metals, to perform the weld, and to communicate the problem and solution to other people. Complex performances go beyond the imitation of discrete skills and require thoughtful problem solving, the integration of knowledge and skills from different disciplines, and the ability to communicate effectively. The documents published by the Secretary's Commission on Achieving Necessary Skills (SCANS, 1991; see Resource B) define clearly the educational changes that must take place in schools to prepare our young people for success in the rapidly changing, technological workplace. We owe it to our teachers to provide them with curriculum models that align with the new requirements for work.

The rapid development of technology, the complexity of the changing workplace, and the explosion of information require that both academic and occupational areas rethink the design of curricula. Living, learning, and working all require a solid foundation of basic skills in reading, writing, speaking, and computing. But the instruction in these basic processes should be broadened beyond the conventional emphases on literature-based reading, creative writing, simple oral presentations, and noncontextual computing.

What kinds of reading, writing, speaking, and mathematical applications are called for in the industries and homes of today and tomorrow? And what about the new basic skill—the use of technology for living, learning, and working? Skill-driven industrial models and conventional academic models continue to ratchet up on their standards. The focus for both should be the development of higher-level, integrated thinking; sophisticated uses of technology; and personally designed performance showing high-quality cognitive and attitudinal dimensions.

The Integrated Concept-Process Model for Secondary and Postsecondary Schools

The integration of content study and process application across academic and occupational curricula, commonly referred to as "school-to-work" curricula, reinforces both academic and occupational learnings and brings greater meaning to their study. The Integrated Concept-Process Model for school-to-work programs uses "integrating concepts"—such as "force," "system," or "equilibrium"—that are drawn from the academic disciplines and occupational areas to focus and align interdisciplinary work.

The focus concept is the lens through which interdisciplinary unit themes are viewed. The purpose of the conceptual lens is to draw thinking above the disciplines to allow for higher-level, integrated thinking as students look for patterns and connections across disciplines. The SCANS competencies are used, as well as discipline-based processes and skills, to integrate and reinforce critical performance abilities across both academic and occupational areas.

The Integrated Concept-Process Model for school to work benefits students in other ways:

- By showing that occupational and academic subjects, in many instances, teach to the same discipline-based concepts through work and knowledge-based examples, students begin to see patterns and connections between core academic and occupational areas.
- By broadening the scope of basic skill applications and relating them to complex performances in working, living, and learning, students move beyond imitation and see relevance as skills are contextualized in work and family roles.
- By teaming in a school-to-work unit, teachers model cooperation and expanded thinking. Students see the value that different perspectives and experiences bring to problem solving and work.

Before a bridge can be built between academic and occupational teachers at the secondary level, however, three things must occur:

1. Misconceptions need to be addressed.
    a. "If I team with an occupational area, I will not have time to teach my subject and will lose academic integrity."

Actually, concept-process integration will reinforce and lead to deeper understanding of discipline-based concepts when students experience their application in broader contexts.

b.   "If I team with academic disciplines, I won't have time to develop my students' work and living skills."

Concept-process integration requires "balance" in school-to-work curricula between teaching for deep understanding and performance-based applications. Generic as well as discipline-based processes and skills are reinforced in a wide variety of academic and occupational living, learning, and working contexts.

c.   "As an academic teacher, my work is very different from the work of an occupational teacher."

Academic and occupational teachers see their work as different because they emphasize different aspects of the curriculum. Occupational teachers value the process side of learning—the doing—and academic teachers focus on the content side of learning—the knowing. Both occupational and academic teachers need a better balance between cognitive and process instructional goals. School-to-work curricula can help create this balance.

2. Curriculum models must be developed that value academic knowledge and occupational skill development, yet bring intellectual rigor and sophisticated performance to both areas.

- What value do concept-process integration models bring to high-level performance in school-to-work curricula?
    a.   Concept-process integration models will raise the curriculum and instruction standards for both the academic and occupational areas. Using content and process activities as a vehicle to gain deep understanding of concepts and conceptual ideas requires a higher level of thinking. Students learn to recognize content as examples of conceptual ideas that transfer to many different situations.
    b.   Defining generic processes as the use of knowledge, skills, attitudes, and task competencies that professional workers display in their organizational roles takes us away from a sole reliance on compartmentalized checklists of technical, employability, and related academic skills. Skills are defined generically as needed to carry out multi-

task assignments in professional decision-making or problem-solving roles.

(Note: "Professional" roles include all jobs where a person solves problems and interacts with others to carry out broader organizational duties in an autonomous fashion; Bailey & Merritt, 1995, p. 26.)

The Integrated Concept-Process Model raises curriculum and instruction standards by insisting on conceptual depth and understanding, and by focusing on the development of skills needed for broad role performances, rather than ending on a note of discrete skills for narrow tasks. When we think of how professionals approach their work, it is not by moving from discrete skill-based task to discrete skill-based task. It is by applying a range of abilities from many different dimensions to complete multidimensional work tasks. This is illustrated by looking at the range of abilities implied in the SCANS competencies: needed resources, needed personnel, interpersonal connections, information required, systems connections, and technology required (SCANS, 1991; see Resource B).

The days of training workers only to the level of discrete skills have passed. All workers need to exhibit more professional-level abilities: complex, systems thinking; independent and teaming abilities; flexibility; autonomous functioning in planning and carrying out complex work assignments; and quality performance in task completion.

3. Concept-process curriculum models must show how the integration process can occur without losing academic integrity or work skill development. How do we maintain academic integrity and quality work skills in concept-process integrated curricula and still achieve the goal of academic and occupational integration?

    a.   Past, and many current, attempts to integrate academic and occupational curricula clash at the topic level. Academic and occupational curricula do not usually integrate at the topic level. By shifting the design focus to the level of integrating concepts, generalizations, and principles, however, the topic problem can be overcome. By selecting a common concept as the integrating lens to attach to the theme of the unit, integration can occur comfortably as a school-to-work unit. For example, the integrating concept of change makes a strong focus lens for the conceptual theme of "A Global Network: The Impact of Changing Technologies in Communication—1800-2000" (Figure 4.2).

b. Many subjects can take part in the above unit on "Changing Technologies." Academic integrity is maintained for each subject by teaching to both discipline-based and specific occupational course concepts through the unit theme, and by applying specific and generalized skills in a meaningful context.

Chart 4.1 provides an excerpt from the Changing Technologies unit that shows how different subjects participating in the unit teach to their own topics, concepts, essential understandings (generalizations), guiding questions, and processes and activities. This ability to integrate around a conceptual theme yet maintain discipline integrity is a critical component in quality integration.

Charts 4.2 through 4.5 show examples of discipline-based concepts that structure the content of academic disciplines.

A curriculum contains both content and process expectations. Teaching to concepts and generalizations (essential understandings) through content ensures intellectual and academic integrity. Essential questions send students on the search for the essential understandings—the deeper, transferable knowledge. It is the essential understandings that show increasing conceptual development and growth. As students ask questions around each new example of a generalization, they expand their conceptual knowledge base. The generalizations become more sophisticated and show greater conceptual complexity as students consider each new example. The generalizations structure the deeper knowledge of a discipline or course. The essential questions systematically guide the development of thinking between the factual and conceptual levels.

Students engage with the essential questions through complex process performances. The complex performances are based on standards set in the SCANS skills, as well as in discipline-based processes and skills.

In integrated teaching units, skills from academic and work contexts are blended as complex performance requirements. The SCANS skills are helpful here because they focus on complex performance and requisite skills. For example, "Identifies, organizes,

(text continues on p. 118)

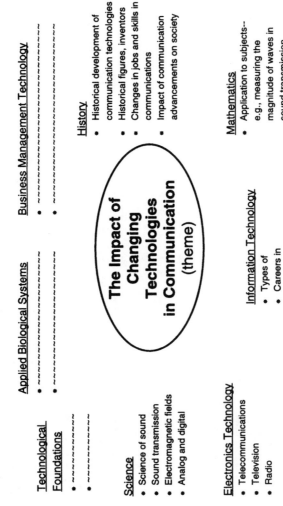

Change

(Integrating concept)

Technological
Foundations
• --------------
• --------------

Applied Biological Systems
• ----------------------
• ----------------------

Business Management Technology
• ---------------------------------
• ---------------------------------

History
• Historical development of communication technologies
• Historical figures, inventors
• Changes in jobs and skills in communications
• Impact of communication advancements on society

Mathematics
• Application to subjects-- e.g., measuring the magnitude of waves in sound transmission

The Impact of Changing Technologies in Communication (theme)

Science
• Science of sound
• Sound transmission
• Electromagnetic fields
• Analog and digital

Electronics Technology
• Telecommunications
• Television
• Radio

Information Technology
• Types of
• Careers in
• Application of information technology

Figure 4.2. Changing Technologies Content Web

Integrating Concept: Change
Unit Theme: "The Impact of Changing Technologies in Communication, 1800–2000"

Course	Topics	Key Concepts	Essential Understandings
Social Studies	Historical Development of Communication Technologies; Historical Figures in Inventions of Communication Technologies; Changes in Jobs Related to Communications	Innovation/invention; evolution; competition; regulation	• New inventions often evolve from earlier models. • Competition may stimulate inventions. • Advancing technology leads to increasing system complexity. • Complex systems may seek order through regulation.
Science	The Science of Sound; Sound Transmission	Waves; wavelength; amplitude; absorption; transfer; induction; sound production; volume; tone; analog; digital	• Sound waves may be amplified. • Magnetic force fields can distort sound.
Electronic Technology	Comparative Communication Technologies	Analog; digital; current; circuit impedance; amplification; voltage slope; transistor; capacitor	• Configuration of technology should be related to task requirements, cost-benefits, and flexibility of use.
Information Technology	Information Technology; Careers; Technologies; Applications	Concepts from art, psychology, science, and economics	• Information may be structured to meet different purposes and to obtain different results.
Mathematics	(Math is applied across all subjects as a process to extend understanding of concepts.)	Range; volume; slope; congruence; resistance; series; impedance	• Amplifying the current in a circuit increases the voltage slope.
English/ Language Arts	(English is applied across all subjects as processes in the activities/ performances.)		• Communication strategies are used to work and learn.
Media/ Literature	(Media/literature supports the thematic study.)		

Chart 4.1. Changing Technologies Planning Chart

Course	Guiding Questions	SCANS/Processes/Skills	Activities/Performances
Social Studies	What kinds of abilities and skills to inventors exhibit? Where do inventors get their ideas for new inventions? How do inventors draw on knowledge from science, art, or other disciplines for their work? What are the dilemmas facing society as a result of advancing technologies? How do systems (e.g., businesses or social systems) deal with increasing complexity?		
Science	How is sound transmitted? How is sound amplified? What is "static"? How does analog differ from digital?	SCANS: • Participate as a team member. • Acquire and organize information. • Communicate information. • Troubleshoot equipment.	1. As a two-person team, disassemble a sound-producing technology and identify the part functions. 2. Draw and label the parts on a chart. 3. Prepare an oral presentation explaining how sound works. 4. Repair a broken radio.
Electronic Technology Information Technology	How do various careers in information technology use communication technology? How does sound affect people? How do careers make use of sound to achieve their goals?	SCANS: • Manage resources.	1. Considering your audience, as an advertising specialist for radio technology, develop a 60-second radio spot for a new product. Consider psychology concepts as you work to "grab" your audience.
Mathematics	How is voltage slope determined? How is mathematics used in different communications careers (e.g., sound technician, audiologist)?		
English/ Language Arts Media/ Literature	What is the purpose of the communication? Who is the audience? (Questions explore the unit themes of selected literature/media.)		

Chart 4.1. Changing Technologies Planning Chart, continued

Number	Slope	Unit of	Risk
Proportion	Equivalence	measure	Sampling
Ratio	Symmetry	Line	Function
Scale	Shape	Point	Variable
Probability	Congruence	Correlation	Prediction
Perimeter	Area	Chance	Angle
Rate	Fractions	Volume	Percent
Domain	Range	Decimals	Average
Ordered pairs	Coordinates	Central	Symbols
Vectors	Expression	tendency	Odds
Rates of change	Intersection	Series	Perspective
Rotation	Distribution	Trends	Relative
		Orientation	magnitude
		Properties	

Chart 4.2. Mathematics Discipline–Based Concepts

Matter	Ecosystem	Development	Order
Energy	Diversity	System	Structure
Transfer	Population	Traits	Interaction
Force/power	Equilibrium	Behaviors	Interdependence
Motion	Reproduction	Similarities	Substance
Model	Fertilization	Differences	Change
Behavior	Heredity	Mass	Conductivity
Evolution	Mutation	Distance	Volume
Organism	Cycle	Temperature	Magnetism
Cell	Scale	Heat flow	Sound
Properties	Action/	Speed	transmission
Environment	reaction	Density	Relative
	Identity		distance
			Patterns

Chart 4.3. Science Discipline–Based Concepts

plans, and allocates resources" is a complex performance that cuts across both occupational and academic areas. To use this complex performance in work and living contexts, the learner would develop skills related to the use of "time," "money," "materials and facilities,"

Culture	Role/status	Leadership	Freedom
Similarities/	Patterns	Government	Equality
differences	Conflict/	Limits	Citizenship
Perspective	cooperation	Transportation	Policy
Behavior	Traditions	Communica-	Supply/
Identity	Laws/rules	tion	demand
Needs/wants	Interdepen-	Groups,	Incentives
Time	dence	institutions	System
Change/	Common good	Origin	Barter
continuity	Rights/respon-	Ethics, values,	Exchange
Location/place	sibilities	and beliefs	Markets
Space/regions	Environment	Customs	Consumption
Resources	Power	Influence	
	Order	Justice	

Chart 4.4. Social Studies Discipline–Based Concepts

Movement	Harmony	Tempo	Action
Rhythm	Dramatization	Tone color/	Aesthetic
Balance	Imitation	timbre	Space
Pattern	Synchronicity	Image	Time
Variation	Imagination	Sound	Energy
Technique	Repertoire	Movement	Interpretation
Expression	Value	Composition	Fluency
Color	Texture	Craftsmanship	Originality
Shape	Space	Structure	Elaboration
Line	Angle	Critique	Flexibility
Form	Tone	Change	Style
Melody	Pitch	Mood	Character
		Function	

Chart 4.5. The Arts Field–Based Concepts

and "human resources." This particular performance would integrate well into the unit on "Changing Technologies" presented previously for the subject areas of family and consumer science, social studies, business education, and technology education.

School-to-Work Integration
in the Elementary School

Preparing students for living, learning, and working in the 21st century requires a coordinated and systematic curriculum design from kindergarten through postsecondary education. "Working smart" in curriculum design and teaching means systematically spiraling key concepts through the grades with developmentally appropriate, related content. As students revisit the concepts and question and investigate the related content through complex performance and activities, they build increasing conceptual depth and understanding.

Elementary students experience academically based content in history, geography, and literature, just as do secondary and postsecondary students. But the elementary level of schooling also needs to broaden the paradigm of content and process instruction. Many elementary schools around the country are already making changes to meet the challenges of the 21st century. They are finding ways to bring computers and enhanced technologies into the instructional program for students. They realize that students need exposure to the many career areas that will be prevalent in their future. We see students exposed to careers through invited speakers, field trips, and some career study. Elementary-grade curricular and instructional designs for the 21st century make certain that students systematically attain the requisite knowledge and skills for success and employability.

Figure 4.3 shares an excerpt from a fifth-grade unit that reinforces school-to-work learnings. Notice that the essential understandings and questions allow students to explore important concepts and principles related to social and economic concepts.

This means that it is not enough to simply list the conventional process skills for learning how to read, write, listen, speak, view, and interact. These abilities must be applied in much broader contexts— even in the elementary grades. Integrating the SCANS competencies into the process performances of instructional units will facilitate the use of these skills in increasingly complex demonstrations at the secondary and postsecondary levels. We cannot afford to wait until secondary school to begin broadening students' process abilities.

At this time, we are graduating many students who will not be able to compete in a global labor market. A major problem is weak performance in basic literacy skills of reading, writing, speaking, viewing, listening, computing, and thinking. Why do we have so

Focus Concept	Grade Level	Unit Theme		Essential Understandings	Essential Questions
Interrelationships	5	Community & Production in the United States		• Advances in technology create new opportunities for communities.	• How do advances in technology create new economic opportunities?

Content Web:

Social Studies

(History)
- ❖ Agricultural to industrial production
- ❖ The knowledge age: New skills for a global economy
- ❖ Community interrelationships

(Economics)
- ❖ Economic stability
- ❖ Production and consumption
- ❖ Global economics
- ❖ Scarcity, supply and demand

(Government)
- ❖ The market economy
- ❖ Regulating trade and commerce
- ❖ Current issues

Mathematics
- ❖ Community production web: percentages
- ❖ Economic charts and graphs
- ❖ Employment changes
- ❖ Production and consumption
- ❖ Projections: trade; employment
- ❖ Estimations

Science
- ❖ Technology and production/distribution
- ❖ The science of production and distribution
- ❖ Inventions

Entrepreneurship
- ❖ The reality of "downsizing" business
- ❖ The rise of entrepreneurs and small businesses
- ❖ Knowledge, skills, and abilities

Occupational
- ❖ Community and industry
- ❖ Types of industry
- ❖ Support for community
- ❖ Use of resources:
- ❖ Geographical data
- ❖ Community interrelationships for production and distribution
- ❖ Specific case studies
- ❖ Changing work competencies

Language Arts
- ❖ Relating interpersonally
- ❖ Communicating messages
  - Speaking
  - Writing
- ❖ Communicating with technology

(Circle in center: Community and Production in the United States (theme))

Essential Understandings
- • Advances in technology create new opportunities for communities.
- • Increased global interaction leads to complex social, political, and economic relationships.
- • Communities cooperate to produce and distribute goods and services.
- • Production rates reflect trends of supply and demand.
- • Entrepreneurs develop markets by meeting or creating needs in a society.
- • Technology expands the forms of communication.
- • Industries depend on human and natural resources for quality production.
- • Inventions range from simple to complex.

Essential Questions
- • How do advances in technology create new economic opportunities?
- • How does international trade affect economic and political relationships?
- • Why do relationships become more complex as global interaction increases?
- • How do communities try to respond to growing complexity in trade?
- • How do communities cooperate to produce and distribute goods and services?
- • What is an "entrepreneurial spirit?"
- • How do entrepreneurs differ from Industrial Age factory workers?
- • How can technology enhance communication?
- • How do resources affect production?
- • How can an invention be protected?

Figure 4.3. Community/Production Unit Excerpt

many students reaching the middle school level still weak in these skills? There are many outside reasons, but there are also many school-based reasons. In too many schools, students are passed from grade to grade with the hope that the next teacher can make greater gains. But students slide through and often slip out at the junior or senior high level, or they graduate with a "seat time" diploma. Addressing the basic SCANS foundational skills with a greater degree of developmental mastery is an elementary-grade necessity.

Our first priority in education is to develop sound literacy skills. All the career exploration in the world won't compensate for a lack of reading, communication, or thinking abilities. If elementary schools red-flag all students who are developmentally delayed in the basic skills, intervention programs making creative use of school personnel and programs can bring greater degrees of student success. When instructional programs are not working for some students, they deserve a more appropriate curriculum. If the amount of time spent on literacy development is not producing the expected level of mastery, then the time devoted to these areas needs to be expanded. Schools can no longer afford to let students slide through, even if outside reasons make the inside instruction difficult.

Unless we make dramatic educational change, only the top fraction of our student population will be truly competitive. This select group will have the requisite education and job performance skills. Students without a college education will be competing with workers from around the world for scarce jobs. Workers from other countries work for much lower wages, as evidenced by the number of U.S. businesses exporting piecework, or even manufacturing plants, to other countries. The result of this labor shift is a shrinking middle class and a burgeoning lower class in the United States. Adding to the dilemma of a global labor market is the fact that technological innovations, such as robotics, will continue to replace many labor positions in developing, as well as in industrialized, nations.

The public needs to be informed that the 21st century requires a higher standard for curriculum and instruction. This standard includes the development of critical and creative thinking; the ability to put knowledge to use in complex living, learning, and working performances; and an instructional program that gives teachers flexibility in engaging students with process and skill development.

The United States has a responsibility to educate its citizens and future citizens to the new standards and requirements. The equitable distribution of computers and technology into all schools should be a national concern and priority. School districts can systematically design curricula to integrate and focus on needed knowledge, processes, skills, and attitudes, but teachers have a right to expect the time and training to design curricula; learn new teaching methods and technologies; and collaborate in school, business, and home partnerships.

Summary

For the past 8 to 10 years, many high schools and middle schools have been working to bridge the demarcation between core academic and occupational education areas. This attempt to provide more integrated school-to-work programming has had its challenges. Although there are a number of schools that feel they have developed a successful model, many are still floundering.

A major problem in creating interdisciplinary teams that include academic and the vocational areas is that they have traditionally approached their instruction in very different ways. It is difficult to find common ground when academic areas focus on content in instruction, and vocational areas focus more on the process, or "doing," side of the curriculum.

To maintain the integrity of both academic and vocational areas in the development of integrated programming, a concept-process model can work effectively. This curricular and instructional transition would require both areas to work toward a higher standard.

A concept-process integrated curriculum model requires that academic and occupational areas identify the concepts that are associated with the topics taught in their respective courses. Interdisciplinary teaching teams, composed of both academic and occupational teachers, then look for common concepts. These concepts provide the "bridge" for building an integrated unit of study. Concepts that are developed through the content of an academic course are exemplified and contextualized in the occupational areas. Appropriate unit themes focus the study around a compatible topic of study viewed through a common conceptual lens. Other important concepts are taught as "topics" in the courses participating in the unit.

The elementary grade levels realize the importance of developing to standard not only the basic skills of reading, writing, listening, speaking, viewing, mathematics, and technology, but also the expanded basics as defined in the SCANS competencies. The expanded basics address those process abilities that will be critical for success in the 21st-century workplace, such as interpersonal skills, leadership, accessing and use of resources, and quality task completion.

This chapter relates the steps presented in Chapter 3 for designing concept-based units to the school-to-work movement. Chapter 5 shares thoughts from teachers on concept-process curricula, provides a variety of unit examples from across the country, and discusses some of the issues related to implementing concept-process curricula in the classroom.

⟪ 5 ⟫

Tips From Teachers:
Creating Concept-Process
Integrated Units

Teachers Speak Out—
The Concept-Process Curriculum and Instruction

The concept-process curriculum and instruction was an emphasis in the United States during the 1960s and early 1970s, largely as a result of the work and research of Hilda Taba (1966). At the same time, the "open classroom" phenomenon was in high gear. Classroom walls came down, teachers teamed, and "creativity" became a popular goal for student learning. As with so many innovations in education, however, the implememtation of open classrooms rode the pendulum of change too far, and curriculum lost its structure. Activities and the quest for creativity replaced a thoughtful structure for knowledge and understanding. Hilda Taba passed away in the mid-1970s, about the time that a backlash was developing against open classrooms. This backlash, referred to as the behaviorist era, required specific, testable objectives that removed the element of subjectivity as much as possible from assessment and evaluation. This focus on objectivity and specificity came at a cost to the development of complex thinking for both teachers and students. When assessments target isolated bits of information and skills, then the standard for teaching and learning follows suit.

There was a period in the early 1980s when educators realized the need for critical thinking skills, and a variety of thinking-skill programs was developed. But in most cases these programs required direct instruction on thinking skills as an adjunct to the daily curricular program. Thinking was decontextualized.

Across the country today, teachers and administrators realize that the ability to think critically and creatively is paramount, and that curriculum designs must support this higher cognitive standard within the context of the teaching-learning environment. In response, educators across the country are working to learn, design, and implement concept-process curriculum models. They realize that to teach students how to think requires continual development of one's own thinking ability. Designing curricula to develop thinking is hard work; teaching students to think is even harder work.

Following are some current reactions and reflections on concept-process education from teachers around the country. This section opens with a letter from a high school mathematics teacher.

> Since our meeting I have been thinking about the teaching of concepts in secondary mathematics. I realized that many math teachers seldom, if ever, teach mathematical conceptual understanding. For some reason the teaching of skills and symbolic manipulation has become the exclusive activity of many math classrooms—while teaching students to think mathematically, and to use mathematics to describe and model the world around them has too often been ignored.
>
> For many years I perfected the teaching of math skills and avoided teaching students the deeper thinking involved with mathematics. Fortunately, The National Council of Teachers of Mathematics Standards reawakened in me the joy that I had felt exploring mathematical ideas as a child. I remember cutting graph paper into various shapes and discovering the concept of area. I remember exploring patterns in logarithmic tables and making the connection between those self-discovered patterns and an understanding of how my slide rule worked. It was the patterns, the themes, the beauty and the art of mathematics that drew me to it, not the symbols and the rote practicing of procedures. As tools of technology replace the manipulative skills of mathematics, there is an even greater need to focus on the applications of mathematics.

The concept of mathematical modeling should be prevalent in our classes. The language of algebra, with its symbolic manipulations and procedures, is one way that we can model physical phenomena and make predictions about the world around us. But there are also graphical and numerical ways to perform the same types of analysis. The theme of algebraic, numerical, and graphical modeling forms a powerful triad for allowing students to probe the world around them.

One of the most powerful tools of mathematics is the concept of slope. When data are portrayed graphically, patterns in the data can often be easily observed. One of the simplest patterns occurs when the data are linear. On the first day of my math classes I have my students walk in front of a motion detector, a device that measures their distance from the detector as a function of time. As the students walk away from, or toward the detector they see a graph plotted of their distance from the detector at each instant in time. If they walk at a steady pace, the graph is a line. The line slopes up when they move away from the detector and down when they move towards it. The faster they move, the steeper the line. It is the measure of the steepness of the line that we call "slope." Students understand the generalization that the "slope of the line is a mathematical model of speed." When students vary their pace the graphs become even more interesting. If they are walking away from the motion detector at an increasing rate, the graph curves upward. If they are slowing down the graph curves a different way. They soon recognize that in the graphical display is contained all of the information they need to analyze the motion of the person who created the graph. They can predict the direction of the motion, the speed of the motion, and whether the person was speeding up or slowing down.

The slope of a graph at a particular point is a measure of the instantaneous rate of change of the object creating the graph. This conceptual and essential understanding transfers to the study of all types of rates of change: rate of speed, typing rate, reaction rate, etc. Whenever we use terms like miles per hour, feet per second, miles per gallon, words per minute, vibrations per second, revolutions per minute, moles per liter, we are treading on the concept of instantaneous rate of change. This is the concept which is referred to as the derivative in calculus.

This one simple activity has led us deep into a fundamental concept underlying differential calculus. I have found that other concepts of mathematics can be introduced in just such a visual and intuitive way. My students actively explore the concepts of mathematics (as well as skills). Though the skills are essential to quality performance, I look forward to curriculum integration to also help my students apply and experience the power of mathematics in authentic, real-world situations offered by the other disciplines.

—SCOTT HENDRICKSON
ALPINE SCHOOL DISTRICT
AMERICAN FORK, UTAH

This teacher shows clearly the understanding of concept-process curriculum planning. He uses the content and applications of mathematics to develop key concepts and the conceptual, transferable understandings of mathematics. He teaches to the conceptual idea through focused, engaging, and relevant applications. Also evident in this letter is the teacher's enthusiasm for instruction. By bringing his own intellectual thought, creativity, and planning to the curriculum and instruction, he is personally rewarded by the interest and progress of his students.

Another letter from a third-grade teacher in Palos Park, Illinois shows the power of concept-based teaching in the elementary grades:

My students are making many connections with the "big ideas" that we have created from in-depth studies. Since September, we have been learning about, discussing, and finding examples of the concept of "perspective" through our literature. A comparison chart (Chart 5.1) helps the children understand the concept. We have read many books and have recorded our thoughts on the chart under the headings of "title, issue, characters, perspectives, outcome, and analysis." The children refer to the chart often and identify perspectives. They also transfer the idea and use the word appropriately across the curriculum in our discussions. I see deep understanding occurring for most students. For example, after reading a biography about Benjamin Franklin that told of the conflict between Franklin and his son William over loyalty

Literature	Issue	Characters	Perspectives	Outcome	Big Idea
Benjamin Franklin, Extraordinary Patriot	Freedom from England	Benjamin Franklin William Franklin	• Benjamin Franklin thought the colonists should be free from England. • William Franklin thought the colonists should stay loyal to England.	Benjamin Franklin and his son William were torn apart in their relationship.	Different perspectives can create conflict.
The Year of the Panda	Saving the panda	The farmers The government	• The farmers thought they should be able to keep their land. • The government thought the farmers should give up their land to grow bamboo for the panda.	Some farmers moved off their land, and others kept their land.	Similarities and differences in perspectives exist among people within the same culture.
Yang the Youngest and His Terrible Year	Practicing the violin	Yang Yang's father	• Yang thought he should be able to practice baseball instead of the violin. • Yang's father thought Yang should practice the violin.	Mr. Connors talked to Yang's father and convinced him that practicing baseball was as important as practicing the violin.	Conflict can be resolved by a change in perspective. Communication can cause a change in perspective.

Chart 5.1. Developing Big Ideas on Perspectives, Grade 2

SOURCE: Marianne Kroll, Palos Community Consolidated School District 118, Palos Park, Illinois. Used by permission.

to the colonies, a student made a connection for our perspective chart, "Different perspectives can cause conflict."

I also see my students asking more intelligent questions in our studies, such as, "Could the colonists have gone back to live in England if they had wanted to?" "What benefit were the colonists getting for the taxes they paid the British?" (We had learned about the concept of "benefit" when we studied one of our units explaining why the Spanish kept coming to the New World while the Vikings didn't.) "Why were the French going to help the colonists in the Revolutionary War when they had fought against them in the French and Indian War?" Our discussions are lively, and the conceptual focus to our curriculum really challenges my students to think.

—MARIANNE KROLL
PALOS COMMUNITY
CONSOLIDATED SCHOOL
DISTRICT 118
PALOS PARK, ILLINOIS

This kindergarten teacher combines elements of the popular "project approach" with the structure of concept-process curriculum design:

I just completed a unit on Houses with my kindergarten class. Concept-process curriculum design fits nicely into the three phases of this project. By engaging students with a project, in phases, I am able to help them understand the generalizations that frame the unit. As each phase of the project progresses, the study takes on more seriousness for students (Figure 5.1).

We begin by relating stories of the subject matter—in this case, houses. Since the children have a good background in what a house is, and why we have houses, this can be done rather quickly. I have them draw pictures of a house and use this as a "pretest." They draw pictures of houses periodically throughout the unit. I compare the drawings to see what new knowledge they have added. The children ask questions which I write down. When we answer them in our research I write the findings down also. I bring in many nonfiction books about houses around the world, building houses, and families around the

Concept	Grade Level	Unit Theme	Essential Understandings	Essential Questions
Construction	K	People and Their Houses	• The construction of houses requires a variety of jobs. • Climate usually determines the types of houses people live in. • Local resources influence how houses are constructed. • Houses have similarities and differences. • Houses provide protection. • Design affects the durability of houses. • People choose colors and different textures to decorate their homes.	- What kind of home do you live in? - How are homes different? . . . alike? - What kinds of material is your house made of? - How do homes provide protection for families? - Why do some houses have to be made stronger than other houses? - How do people decorate their homes? - Where do the materials to make a home come from? - What kinds of jobs are there in constructing a house?

Content Web:

Mathematics
• Number
• Measuring
• Shapes
• Patterns
• Graphing
• Counting
• Sorting
• Classifying
• Money

Health
• Safety
 - tools
 - work site

Science
• Weather
• Materials
• Systems

Art
• Size
• Shape
• Color
• Texture

(People and Their Houses)

Music
• Working to music
 - melody
 - rhythm
 - tempo

Literature
• Nonfiction: how-to books
• Fiction: homes
• Multimedia: homes and how to build them

Figure 5.1. House Construction Web

SOURCE: Mary Russell, East Valley School District, Spokane, Washington. Used with permission.

world. I use all the versions of the *Three Little Pigs*. A new version has high-tech houses! Our purpose for reading the different versions changes as we evaluate the choices for home building materials.

I also read lots of books about families. These books, along with the discussions and activities, address many of the generalizations. I bring in as many experts as I can find. This year one of my student's fathers owns a window business. He brought in samples of windows and brochures for the children. He told them how glass was made and the process for making windows. The children turned the rice table into a glass factory. Another father is a plumber. Students were building water systems and drawing diagrams of their creations. We looked at blueprints and they made their own. These children also experienced the firestorm and many lost their homes and had to rebuild. I think that makes housebuilding even more relevant for these students.

We went for a walk and looked at houses in the neighborhood. I call this our field study. I give the students clipboards and assign groups specific things to look for on the walk. Roof types, window shapes, garages, siding types, etc. They draw pictures and when we get back we share the findings. These observations are essential understandings such as, "House construction uses many different shapes," or "Roof and siding materials have different textures." Through these activities the children realize the importance of the various concepts in curricular areas because they need them to work on the project. If your job is to describe window shapes you had better know them! I get more comments from parents about this. Their children bug them to learn at home, because they need the information and skills to help them build the class house.

The actual building of the house happens many weeks after the beginning of the unit. The children sign up for a construction job. They look at books and ask the professionals how to do the job. I give them real saws, tape measures, paint brushes, pipes, etc. I make it as real as I can and still maintain safety. We use wiring, fuse boxes, outlets, hot water tank, wallpaper, tile roof, shingle roof, rain gutters, and window boxes. Sometimes you have to use your imagination to really see the item, but it is there.

We had a piece of carpeting, but it was too big for the house. The "carpet layers" tried to measure the floor with a yardstick, but the stick was too big. I asked them to think about the things in our room which could be used to measure. They looked around and finally found the unifix cubes (which is what I had hoped they would find). They hooked the cubes together into two lines for width and depth. They laid them out onto the carpet and drew the lines (I cut the carpet!). They counted each row of cubes and wrote them down so they could report back to the class. As you can see, they used several mathematical concepts and also gained some of the essential understandings.

For the generalization "Design affects the durability of houses" I had them make houses out of marshmallows and toothpicks. We had interesting designs but alas—only certain houses remained standing. We analyzed why, and tried the same theories with block houses.

The preceding activities completed phases one and two of the unit. Phase three was sharing and playing. We shared with parents and other classes. Playing in the house is the reward for all the hard work.

You asked me about any insights I might have about helping students understand the importance of concepts. I think it is the connection to real life. You can find real-life applications of concepts within any theme. Connect students with the real-world applications and let them play the required roles. This is especially true for primary children. Any time a child takes on an adult role it is important to him or her. Making the project big in size helps also. I observed the sixth graders looking at our house. They immediately got in and wanted to play. I began to think about the kind of house they would make and the details they could achieve. I almost wanted to move up a few grades! Teachers need to keep the learning as hands-on as possible. Children will naturally read, write, use mathematics skills, etc. if teachers demand they show their understanding of concepts and generalizations in different ways as they work on a big project.

—MARY RUSSELL
PONDEROSA ELEMENTARY SCHOOL
EAST VALLEY SCHOOL DISTRICT
SPOKANE, WASHINGTON

And finally, some general comments from teachers' initial training and implementation efforts in concept-process curriculum design.

Walking into class I thought to myself, "I know all there is to know about writing a unit." (I had learned all the latest in planning and developing integrated lessons.) "This will be an easy credit." Was I surprised! I realized that even though I had been making the connections with my "themes," my students had not. I was missing a key element by not presenting the concept and making certain my students were drawing the connections. I was teaching facts for the sake of knowing facts. I now know I must go back and redevelop my own way of thinking and revise my lessons. This class was a real eye-opener. I think it is not only going to make my students more excited about learning, but will make me more excited about teaching.

—DORIS MADDEN
LAKE WASHINGTON SCHOOL
DISTRICT
REDMOND, WASHINGTON

There is no doubt in my mind . . . that content must be tied directly to a concept or concepts in order for students to assimilate the essential information and skills. At the workshop our sixth grade team was able to breathe life into our somewhat undefined unit on "Ancient Civilizations" by identifying a conceptual lens that would give greater purpose to our students' learning. With "Interconnections" as the lens on our theme of "Ancient Civilizations: Cairo to Canton to King County," our students will be able to relate the past with the present. The introduction of the concept has changed my social studies unit from a memorization of facts into valuable knowledge that will benefit my students for a lifetime. If this sounds a little overly dramatic, or a bit overstated, it is only because I am truly excited about the entirely new perspective I have on relevant and meaningful learning. Students need the basics and a balance in curriculum; but the concept, or "big picture" can make learning truly exciting.

—JODI STUECKLE BARNHART
BEAVERTON SCHOOL DISTRICT
BEAVERTON, OREGON
(PREVIOUSLY: LAKE WASHINGTON
SCHOOL DISTRICT
REDMOND, WASHINGTON)

Teacher-Designed Units

Teachers from around the country are developing concept-based units. Although design formats differ, the units contain common components. Space limitations prohibit the inclusion of entire units in this section, but excerpts share the different unit components. Each excerpt is accompanied by comments pointing out particular strengths.

The kindergarten unit excerpted in Chart 5.2 illustrates the quality of coherence. There is a clear relationship between the essential understandings, the essential questions, and the unit activities. In a coherent design, the questions and activities should develop the essential understandings, as well as the process and skill abilities.

In topically based units, the activities may relate to the topic, but often fail to develop the transferable knowledge. Students are assumed to have reached understandings that even the teacher has not always consciously identified. Making certain that students can relate learning from topics and activities to the "bigger ideas" helps ensure instructional closure. Students understand the relevance of a topic study.

The fourth-grade unit on "Building Community" (Chart 5.3) uses the conceptual lens of "Interdependence" to focus the study. Notice that the essential understandings for this unit are more sophisticated than the kindergarten example. The questions also require more background knowledge. It is the questions that drive instruction rather than a set of verb-driven objectives. The questions engage student interest and are investigated through a variety of activities. Some of the questions and activities relate directly to the community in which the students live; others generalize to the idea of any community.

Chart 5.4 shares a culminating performance for the unit excerpted in Chart 5.3. A scoring guide for one aspect of the performance, the cartoon, is based on three criteria: creativity, craftsmanship, and development of ideas. Notice the use of descriptive terminology to differentiate the four levels of performance (e.g., original, thoughtful, vivid, clear). These terms are more descriptive than words like *sometimes, often,* or *seldom.* It is important for teaching teams to develop clarity on what these terms look like in student work, however, so that they can help students internalize the criteria. Notice also that the "Novice" level is stated in terms of what the students can do, rather than just delineating what students cannot do.

(text continues on p. 139)

Grade 1 Unit
Unit Theme: "It's Off to Work We Go"
Focus Concepts: Community/Work

Essential Understandings	Essential Questions	Processes	Skills	Suggested Activities
People work to meet needs. People work to produce or accomplish something. Community depends on people working together. Location and resources affect the kinds of work people do.	What is work? Why do people work? What kinds of work are done in your family? What kinds of work can children do? Why must people in a community work together? How might where people live affect their work? How do people decide on what kind of work they want to do?	Acquiring/evaluating information Organizing/interpreting information Applying/presenting information Participation in groups	Questioning Listening Group discussion Graphing Noting details Using criteria to develop a product Taking different roles in group work	Brainstorm/chart/graph responses of different kinds of work students do at home or school. Read *I Am Helping* by Mercer Mayer. Have students list the types of work Little Critter did and compare their work. Invite guest speakers to talk about the work they do. Discuss questions.

Chart 5.2. Grade 1 Unit Excerpt

SOURCE: Davenport Community Schools, Davenport, Iowa: Ronda Bird, Corrin Hentzel, Belinda Holbrook, Beth Fitzpatrick-Peters, Joan Herrig, Tammy Murphy-Flynn, Jean Powers. Used by permission.

Grade 4 Unit
Unit Theme: "Building Community"
Focus Concept: Interdependence

Essential Understandings	Essential Questions	Processes	Skills	Suggested Activities
Community members demonstrate interdependence, as well as self-reliance.	• In what ways are community members interdependent? .... • Why is it important for community members to appreciate the unique qualities of self? others?	• Acquiring/evaluating information	• Brainstorming; active listening	• Brainstorm the meaning of community and interdependence. • Create "Topic Tables of Interest"; share 1 minute of information by turn; debrief active listening skills and share unique qualities discovered; discuss essential questions.
Rules and procedures establish and maintain order.	• Why do groups and communities have rules? • Why do we have rules in school? • Why do rules apply to everyone in a group?			
Resolving conflict helps a community operate effectively.	• What is conflict? • What kinds of conflict have you had at school? • What kinds of conflict might be found in a community? • Why does failure to resolve conflict affect a community? • How can conflict be resolved?			

Chart 5.3. "Building Community" Unit Excerpt—Grade 4
SOURCE: Davenport Community Schools, Davenport, Iowa: Deb Kretschmer, Wanda Leonard. Used by permission.

Culminating Performance: Analyze the Truman School community in order to understand how using lifeskills promotes a positive climate for learning. Demonstrate understanding by creating a story about a day in which you used at least four different lifeskills, sequenced in order from the start to the end of the day. Explain how using the lifeskills affected your learning for that day. Present your story in one of three ways:

1. Write your story as a personal narrative.
2. Draw your story in cartoon form.
3. Write your story as a play and perform it in front of an audience.

Scoring Guide for Culminating Performance: Cartoon

Criteria	Excellent	Highly Competent	Competent	Novice
Creativity	Original and thoughtful drawings, consisting of at least four cartoon frames showing the use of lifeskills. Engaging dialogue in each frame.	Original drawings, consisting of four cartoon frames, illustrating the use of lifeskills. Effective dialogue present in each frame.	Drawings, consisting of four cartoon frames, illustrate the uses of lifeskills. Dialogue is present in some cartoon frames.	Drawings, consisting of less than four cartoon frames, illustrate the use of lifeskills.
Craftsmanship	Drawings are vivid, with multiple details to accurately illustrate the story. More than one medium is used to complete the cartoon frames. Meticulous overall appearance.	Drawings are clear, with details that accurately illustrate the story. More than one medium is used to complete the cartoon frames. Neat overall appearance.	Drawings are clear, with some detail added to illustrate the story. One medium is used to complete the cartoon frames. Neat overall appearance.	Drawings attempted to illustrate the story. One medium is used to complete the cartoon frames. Some errors mar overall appearance.
Development	More than four lifeskills developed in the story with reasonable and well-developed examples of each. Thoughtful and accurate explanation of the impact of lifeskills on learning. Engaging beginning, middle, and end to story.	Four lifeskills developed in the story with reasonable examples of each. Detailed explanation of the impact of lifeskills on learning. Effective beginning, middle, and end to the story.	Four lifeskills mentioned in the story with examples of each. Impact of the lifeskills on learning mentioned. Story includes beginning, middle, and end.	Fewer than four lifeskills in the story, with some examples included. Impact of lifeskills on learning not complete. Evidence of a beginning and end to the story.

Chart 5.4. "Building Community" Unit Excerpt—Grade 4—Culminating Performance and Sample Scoring Guide

SOURCE: Davenport Community Schools, Davenport, Iowa: Deb Kretschmer, Wanda Leonard. Used by permission.

Beginning, or developmentally delayed, learners deserve to know what they can do even if their work is at a lower level. They also need to know the next steps for their learning. Parents need to be clear on the actual developmental level of the student work, but they also deserve to hear what their child has accomplished.

Sixth-grade teachers in Palos Park, Illinois are working on a unit related to ancient Rome (Figure 5.2). They are using the conceptual lens of political and economic systems to focus the study. Essential understandings go beyond the facts to the transferable level, and the critical content related to the study of ancient Rome provides the foundation for helping students connect new knowledge with old knowledge. Teachers use essential questions to help students learn to generalize from specific examples to transferable understandings.

The high school unit excerpted in Chart 5.5 uses measurement, tools, and experimental design to build a floatable boat. Students use geometric relationships and algebraic notation. They also manipulate expressions and solve equations as they find area and volume in the shapes of their boat. Students apply the concepts of buoyancy and displacement to the real-life performance of finding how much weight a floating boat can hold.

Notice that the essential understandings for the unit excerpted in Chart 5.5, which were drawn from the district curriculum frameworks, are very general and would be considered Level 1 generalizations. They are moved to Levels 2 and 3 through the use of the essential questions in the second column. Can you find examples of more sophisticated generalizations embedded within the essential questions?

The following unit excerpt was developed by teachers in Gloucester, Massachusetts for high school students. Although they teach the topic of the American Revolution using directed questions and activities, they also teach beyond the facts and develop essential understandings related to the general concept of "revolution." The American Revolution offers critical content knowledge related to past history, but it also serves as a tool for teaching to deeper, conceptual understandings.

UNITED STATES HISTORY

Topic: American Revolution
Focus concepts: Revolution and Change

(text continues on p. 143)

Subject Area: _____ Social Studies

Concept	Grade	Unit Theme	Essential Understandings	Essential Questions
Systems	6	Ancient Rome: Political, Economic, and Social Systems	• The resources of a region determine types of food, clothing, and shelter. • Political systems organize citizenry to maintain order and achieve societal goals. • Economic systems structure choices about how goods and services are distributed. • Cultural values and perspectives influence the architecture of historical periods and groups.	- How do societies organize to meet their basic needs? - Why do societies create political systems? Why do these systems differ across cultures and through time? - How did supply and demand influence Roman market choices? - How does supply and demand affect global trade today?

Content Web:

Math
• Roman numerals
• Resource economics
• Word problems

Literature/Media
• Mythology/fables
• Videos
• CD-interactive
• Expository reading
• Narrative reading

Fine Arts
• Architecture: line, form
• Period craft: shape, technique,
• Period art: pattern...

Ancient Rome: Political, Economic, and Social Systems

Social Studies
• Geographic location
  - Food
  - Shelter
  - Clothing
  - Technology
  - Transportation
• Art
• Religion
• Traditions
• Medicines
• Language
• Sociopolitical organization
• Branches of government

Figure 5.2. Social Studies Content Web

SOURCE: Donna Clark, Gina Mannino, Prudee Topielec, Mark Sandusky: Palos Consolidated Community School District 118, Palos Park, Illinois. Used with permission.

Grade 9/10 Unit
Unit Theme: "Float That Barge"
Subject Areas: Applied Physics and Mathematics

Essential Understandings	Essential Questions	Critical Content	Processes	Skills
Properties, Measurement, Scale • Measurement expresses properties on a numerical scale. • Scale is a range of possible values for a measured property that allows comparison of objects, systems, or events. **Number sense** • Linear and nonlinear measurements use a variety of number types.	**Properties, Measurement, Scale** • How do the density and mass of a floating object affect its buoyancy? • How are density and mass measured? • How does the ratio of a floating object's mass to its volume impact decisions related to water transportation? • Why are the area, pressure, volume, and displacement measured in different ways? • How is the variable of density treated when measuring the degree of displacement for a floating object?	**Physical Science** • Forces (e.g, buoyancy, gravity) • Measurement • Density • Displacement **Algebra** • Variables and expressions • Linear and nonlinear equations • Formulas • Rational expressions and operations **Geometry** • Area/length/volume formulas • Geometric properties	• Select instruments and techniques to gather and synthesize useful information. • Develop and practice multiple thinking and problem-solving strategies. • Offer plausible explanations for disparities in data. • Set and work toward standards for quality work.	• Select and use direct and indirect formulas for length, area, and volume. • Apply mathematical calculations in quantifying scientific data. • Apply formulas for density and mass. • Use algebraic notation to solve for variable. • Assess conclusions in relation to other sources and discuss the limitations and conclusions. • Reflect on and adjust work related to standards criteria.

Chart 5.5. Mathematics/Physics Unit Excerpt—Grades 9 and 10

SOURCE: Lisa C. Dodd, Juanita High School, Lake Washington School District, Redmond, Washington. Used by permission.

141

Essential Understandings	Essential Questions	Critical Content	Processes	Skills
Measurement • All measurement involves error and uncertainty. • Length, area, and volume of geometric shapes are represented through specific formulas.	**Number sense** • Why do methods used to solve linear or nonlinear situations incorporate a variety of number types? **Measurement** • How do the attributes of geometric figures determine the choice of measuring tools? • How can error be minimized? • How are formulas for length, area, and volume of shapes the same and different?			

Chart 5.5. Mathematics/Physics Unit Excerpt—Grades 9 and 10, continued

SOURCE: Lisa C. Dodd, Juanita High School, Lake Washington School District, Redmond, Washington. Used by permission.

Critical Content: The American Revolution

- Taxes and tariffs
- Colonial opposition
- Major figures
- Major battles

Generalizations (Essential Understandings)

- Revolution results from dissatisfaction with the existing political, economic, social, or religious order.
- Revolution can result from rigidity in an existing system.
- Revolution can lead to a dramatic change in the social, economic, political, or religious order.
- Political revolution is often characterized by the use of violence on the part of one or both sides in an attempt to block stated goals.
- "Radical" political leaders use a variety of propaganda techniques to create extreme reactions.
- Revolutions feature charismatic leaders who inspire, lead, and coalesce factions involved in change movements.

Essential Questions

1. What factors led to the American Revolution?
2. How did the principles of freedom and independence forge the revolutionary movement?
3. Why were the Americans victorious?
4. How did the American Revolution affect the politics, economy, and society of the developing nation in the late 1700s and early 1800s?
5. Why were the American Revolution and the resulting institutions and practices of government central to the foundation of the American political system?
6. How does the U.S. Constitution and the Bill of Rights protect the principles and ideals of an American representative democracy?

7. Why do revolutions often result in violence? How does "rigidity" in a social, political, or economic system affect the functioning of the system?

8. How might conflict be resolved other than through violence?

9. Why do leaders emerge during revolutions? What are the characteristics of revolutionary leaders?

10. Are revolutions always political/social? What other kinds of revolutions have occurred in American society? How has the computer revolution affected American society? Who are the leaders of the computer revolution? How are they alike and different from political revolutionary leaders?

Suggested Activities

- Create a timeline of key events for the American Revolution.
- Analyze the Declaration of Independence as a manifesto upon which the American Revolution was based.
- In cooperative groups, generate "revolutionary ideas" that could become catalysts for change in our society today.
- Research and present an autobiographical sketch of a major figure of the American Revolution.

Performance Task

WHAT: Compare a key figure in the American Revolution to the leader of one other revolution in past or current history . . .

WHY: in order to realize the power and characteristics of charismatic leaders.

HOW: Demonstrate understanding by writing a clear and insightful essay comparing and contrasting the characteristics of the two leaders and illustrating how they influenced and shaped the ideals and direction of the revolutions.

Other Forms of Assessment

- Objective tests and quizzes on basic knowledge of the American Revolution

- Alternative assessments, such as projects, interviews, and debates to demonstrate deeper understandings related to the concepts of "revolution and change"

—JOHN T. KEARNS, JANELL ANDREWS,
GRETA H. KENNEDY
GLOUCESTER HIGH SCHOOL,
GLOUCESTER, MASSACHUSETTS

The probability unit in the following excerpt highlights the conceptual understandings of mathematics. Students engage with the process skills and "do" mathematics, but the teacher makes certain that the essential understandings are stated clearly in the unit. Teaching is inductive. Teachers do not assume that students understand the conceptual ideas of mathematics. They make certain that understanding is demonstrated beyond rote performance.

MATHEMATICS

Course: Introduction to Algebra
Conceptual Theme: Probability
Concepts: Probability, ratio, proportion, measurement, independent and dependent events, permutations

Generalizations (Essential Understandings)

- Proportions use ratios to compare data.
- Proportions convert measurements.
- The probability of an event is a ratio between 0 and 1.
- Independent and dependent events determine the type of experiment.
- A permutation creates ordered arrangements.

Essential Questions

- How do we set up two ratios to make a proportion?
- How do we convert a ratio in one measurement into another?
- Why is it necessary to convert measures from one unit to another?
- Why do units have to correspond in a proportion?

- What procedures are necessary in order to find the probability of an event occurring?
- Why is the probability always between 0 and 1?
- How do we classify an event as either independent or dependent?
- How do permutations help to find the number of possible outcomes?

Activities

- Given two ratios comparing the same event from two separate bodies, determine if they are a proportion.
- Collect data in a particular area and use theoretical probability to make conclusions.
- Use coins or dice to find the sample space and the probability of the event occurrence.
- Create a new event, categorize the event as either independent or dependent, and calculate the probability.

Performance Task

WHAT: Experiment with situations having a certain number of outcomes . . .

WHY: in order to predict a given outcome based on theories of probability.

HOW: Demonstrate understanding by tossing a coin or rolling a die and predicting outcomes. Explain your reasoning.

—HOGAN GUIDER
GLOUCESTER HIGH SCHOOL
GLOUCESTER, MASSACHUSETTS

Note that the essential questions and activities for the probability unit are designed to help students develop conceptual understanding. The performance task uses a formula that states "why" students are to perform experiments. The demonstration of understanding stated in the "how" statement requires that students do more than predict outcomes. They must explain the reasoning for the predictions, which will show that they can relate the predictions to the theories of probability.

Mathematics teachers state in workshops that they know the conceptual ideas that underlie the skill-based performances, but they find it difficult to translate the numeric representation of ideas into sentence form. But many students do not understand "why" mathematical applications work in different contexts. Clearly stating the conceptual generalizations and principles of mathematics will help those students who need the support of the English language to bridge from application to understanding. Another benefit of stating the conceptual ideas that underlie the applications of mathematics is to show the development of related mathematical ideas from the elementary through postsecondary school levels.

Another high school unit from a teacher in Gloucester, Massachusetts illustrates how the identification of a range of unit concepts provides options for writing key generalizations. The generalizations are essential conceptual understandings that provide focus for the unit instruction. The essential questions are a combination of "what," "why," and "how" questions that engage students' minds and interest. The activities flow from the questions and lead students to the essential understandings. The performance task requires teachers to identify "why" they want students to engage in the study. The performance must demonstrate this understanding.

ART

Course: Introduction to Painting
Topic: Color/Acrylic Painting
Concepts: Natural and applied color, energy, wavelength, electromagnetic spectrum, radiant energy, light, pigment, reflection, refraction, additive, subtractive, transmission, reception, absorption, visual constructs, functions, systems, classifications, relationships, interactions, combinations, expressionism, impressionism, communication, historical functions, cultural functions, compositional elements

Generalizations (Essential understandings)

- Light sources emit energy that make it possible to see color.
  — Light is a very small portion of the electromagnetic spectrum.

- — Radiant energy traveling through space in the form of waves creates an electromagnetic spectrum.
- — White light traveling through a prism breaks up into a spectrum of colors from red (longer wavelength) to violet (shorter wavelength).
- [Color] vision begins with the eye.
  - — Light of a certain wavelength reflects off the surface of an object, is received by the retina, and is perceived by the brain as color.
- Objects absorb, transmit, and/or reflect light.
- Color is either additive (refracted) or subtractive (reflected).
  - — Additive primaries are green, red, and blue light. From these three additive primaries, most other colors are made.
  - — Green, red, and blue light combine to produce white light.
  - — Acrylic paint and objects have subtractive color because they absorb, transmit, or reflect light.
- The artist uses color as a means of expression, as an organizing principle of design, and for aesthetics.
  - — Impressionistic color represents the closely observed color of an object in actual light.
  - — Expressive color conveys the artist's interpretation of an emotion, belief, or idea.
  - — Color has an emotional effect based on cultural associations and physiological responses.
  - — The color effect of a composition results from the artist's use of color and color combinations.

Essential Questions

- What is color?
- What is the vocabulary of color?
- How does color occur in the natural world?
- How do we perceive color?
- How is color used by the artist?
- How is color used as a design principle to create repetition, variety, rhythm, balance, compositional unity, and emphasis?
- What does the artist's choice of colors tell you about the artist?

- How can color convey ideas, beliefs, or emotions?
- How does an artist's use of color influence you?
- If the colors used by an artist in a painting were changed, would the meaning of the painting be changed? In what ways?

Activities

1. Create four color compositions using colored paper: monochromatic composition, analogous composition, complementary composition, and triad composition.
2. Analyze great works of art and determine how the artist used color to convey ideas, beliefs, or emotions.
3. Investigate cultural influences on personal ideas about the expressive meanings of color.
4. Discuss historical uses of particular colors and the cultural symbolism in their use.
5. Work to control the painting medium by creating an original abstract or figurative work of art that duplicates the color palette used by your chosen artist.
6. Contribute an original painting to a student show.

Sample Performance Tasks

WHAT: Analyze the use of color in works of art . . .

WHY: in order to understand how artists control expression, design, and aesthetics through color.

HOW: . . . by examining a body of work of one artist and presenting findings to the class.

WHAT: Experience the relationship of artist to viewer . . .

WHY: in order to understand how an audience perceives and responds to artistic works.

HOW: . . . by participating in a public showing of personal artwork and writing a reflection paper on audience perceptions and responses.

Resources

- Paintings by Van Gogh, Cezanne, Bacon, Rothko, and Kiyonaga
- Architecture of Egypt, India, Iran, China, and the United States

- *The Art of Seeing,* by Paul Zelanski and Mary Pat Fisher
- *Design and Composition,* by Nathan Goldstein
- *The Visual Arts: A History,* by Hugh Honour and John Felding

—Jacqueline L. Kapp
Gloucester High School
Gloucester, Massachusetts

A middle school unit on Early Humans uses the conceptual lens of "migration/journey." The conceptual lens allows the learnings to transcend the facts related to the topic of early humans and consider ideas related to human migration through time. These transferable understandings can be applied to many different examples. Each example provides deeper conceptual insight, and essential understandings build on each other over time. The subconcepts allow the teacher to identify other important conceptual and transferable understandings.

The teacher draws from the critical content of specific pieces of literature and from the local community to develop foundational knowledge and understanding. But the goal is to teach beyond the facts to the bigger ideas.

SOCIAL STUDIES AND LANGUAGE ARTS

Topic: Early Humans
Focus Concepts: Migration/Journey
Subconcepts: Need, community, civilization, culture, geography, survival, risk

Generalizations (Essential Understandings)

- People migrate in response to a variety of physical, social, psychological, or economic needs.
- There is a relationship between the migration of people and the geography of their environment (the study of the interrelationships between the earth's physical features, living features, and man-made features).
- Migration refers to permanent or seasonal movement of individual people, animals, or whole communities.
- Human populations share a common need for survival.

- Communities form to meet individual and group physical, social, and emotional needs.
- As complex societies, civilizations share similar characteristics (stable food supply, specialization of labor, government, social strata, etc.) and are comprised of smaller communities.
- Migration leads to the spread of ideas and culture.
- Migration and journey involve elements of risk.
- Literature reflects the period, ideas, culture, and outlooks of a community of people living in a particular era.

Essential Questions

- Why did people begin living in communities in earliest times?
- Why did early humans migrate? Why do people migrate today?
- How does geography affect a migration?
- What kinds of needs do we share as the Gloucester community? The broader human community? Our school community? Are these "internal" or "external" needs, and can we define the difference?
- What defines a community? Are there characteristics that are unique to each community? The same?
- What is meant by the "geography" of a community? What is the "culture" of a community? What is the relationship between the geography of Gloucester and the culture of Gloucester? Can we see similar relationships when looking at *Maroo of the Winter Caves*?
- How has the migration of people and their ideas affected the community of Gloucester? What are the similarities between this experience and our study of the migrations of early humans?
- How do historians study the movement of people, and why are their findings important to us today?
- What is the difference between a community and a civilization? What does each of these need to survive?
- What are some of the risks and benefits involved with a migration or a journey?

Sample Activities

1. Study a map of the world from early human history showing glaciers, early settlement areas, and migration routes. In

cooperative groups, discuss a series of questions related to the geography of migration. Can we make any connections between the placement of the glaciers, settlements, and the migration patterns of early humans? Record theories to reconsider later in the unit work.

2. Read, observe, and record evidence, using quotations and page numbers from *Maroo of the Winter Caves,* for the following categories: tools, clothing, beliefs, shelter, communication, food, fire, Ice Age, travel, animals, hunting, and burial practices.

3. Using a variety of reference materials, record findings on a chart for four groups of early humans: Homo Habilus, Homo Erectus, Neanderthal, and Cro-Magnon. Note dates of existence, physical appearance, toolmaking, and ways of dealing with the Ice Age.

4. As a class, brainstorm the meaning of the term *need.* Compare modern and early human needs using a Venn diagram. Discuss common needs and differences. Identify reasons for the differences.

5. View a video on the discovery of the Lascaux Cave Art, and study prints of the cave walls. Discuss why early humans may have decided to create art, and why we create art today.

—LAUREN DE CONSTANT
O'MALEY MIDDLE SCHOOL
GLOUCESTER, MASSACHUSETTS

Teaching Conceptually:
Questions and Answers

*What are some of the biggest problems
with moving from a topically driven model
of instruction to a conceptually driven model?*

- The design of the curriculum heavily affects instruction. A topically based curriculum model reinforces fact-based instruction. As the amount of information to be learned increases in a society, topics receive an increasingly shallow treatment in order to cover the course material. Teachers in a topically based curriculum have been trained to see their job as helping students learn the facts and develop skills through activities related to the topic of study. They use problem solving as a strategy to engage higher-level thinking, but the amount of instructional time spent developing and engaging complex thinking is limited by the traditional design of a curriculum.

To move from a topically driven to a conceptually driven model of curriculum and instruction, we first need to understand the design differences. Chart 5.6 compares some of the key aspects of both models.

Notice that both models value a foundation of specific, fact-based knowledge and skills. The difference lies in the culminating focal point for instruction. Topically based models culminate learning more often with the specific facts, whereas concept-based models culminate learning with the conceptual understandings that can be drawn from the facts.

What classroom strategies and techniques help teachers experience success with this model of curriculum and instruction?

- Teaching to ideas in a classroom brings in the art of teaching. Learning how to create an environmental gestalt brings together the best of what we know about how children learn.
  a. Engaging students in learning through multiple modalities, so aptly described by Howard Gardener with his ideas on "multiple intelligences"
  b. Providing a balanced educational program that draws on individual, cooperative learning and paired learning experiences
  c. Knowing when to lead and when to follow with a balance of direct instruction and student-centered and independent learning
  d. Using a variety of instructional and assessment strategies to engage students—from periodically selecting passion areas of study, to generating essential questions of interest, to self-evaluating according to agreed-upon criteria

Topic-Based Curricular Designs	Concept-Based Curricular Designs
Facts and activities center around a specific topic of study, such as the Industrial Revolution.	Facts and activities center around a specific topic of study, but a conceptual lens forces thinking to higher levels as students consider the "transferable ideas and questions" that derive from the topic of study.
Topic-based objectives drive instruction.	Essential questions that are drawn from both the topic and generalizable levels of knowledge drive instruction.
Curriculum is focused on learning and thinking about specific facts.	Curriculum is focused on using specific facts to understand transferable concepts and ideas.
Content categories and topics provide the curricular structure for Grades K-12.	Discipline-based concepts structure the categories and topics of curriculum for Grades K-12.
Instructional activities focus on specific topics and facts.	Instructional activities focus on specific topics and facts in order to generalize understanding beyond the facts to the conceptual level.
Instructional activities call on a variety of discrete skills.	Instructional activities call on complex performances using a variety of skills.
Curriculum is topic centered.	Curriculum is idea centered.

Chart 5.6. Topic-Based and Concept-Based Curricular Designs

    e.   Developing the art of questioning to engage the minds and hearts of students, flowing from specific to open-ended questions with an artful ear to developing understanding

    f.   Helping students construct meaning through a curriculum and learning environment that encourage pattern seeking and connections at both the concrete and abstract levels

g.   Creatively and critically teaching beyond the facts to help students form mental structures (schema) in the brain for handling new knowledge and relating new knowledge to past knowledge

- Teachers who are beginning to implement concept-process curriculum models are discovering techniques to help students think beyond the facts. With a student population that has been trained to think more about facts than ideas, the transition can be difficult. It takes patience and perseverance on the part of the teachers, but if they persist, students will begin to understand that facts relate to bigger ideas. Illinois teacher Marianne Kroll finds that developing students' understanding of individual concepts, and then having them experience a variety of examples that illustrate a related conceptual idea, allows her to expand students' thinking systematically. In a school district using a concept-based curriculum model for K through 12, the job of instruction becomes easier for teachers because conceptual knowledge and understanding are shaped systematically through the grades, and teachers form a cohesive vertical team.

What "mental paradigms" and attitudes must teachers shift in order to teach more conceptually?

- One of the first issues in conceptual teaching is becoming comfortable with identifying and teaching to abstract ideas. For teachers who have been trained to focus on specific facts, dealing with abstract ideas can be discomfiting. But abstract ideas are the foundation of more lasting and transferable knowledge.
- Concept-process teaching requires that teachers view the fact base not only as important foundational knowledge, but also as a tool for developing deeper understanding of key concepts and conceptual ideas.
- It takes practice to identify the key concepts and deeper lessons and principles to be derived from the study of a specific topic. Because this identification requires teachers to self-question and respond to essential questions around their topic of study, it helps to plan with other teachers to broaden the questioning

and discussion processes. Why are we teaching this topic? What are the important understandings that transcend the facts?

- When teachers hold a "big picture" vision of knowledge, they help students see the patterns, connections, and transferability of knowledge.

- In concept-process curriculum models, teachers understand that content and process have their own criteria for assessment but that they must reinforce each other in the learning process.

- Teachers engage students with complex performances that often draw from multiple modalities and require quality execution of discrete and nested skills.

- Assessment is critical to student improvement. Learning how to develop and evaluate an array of assessment tools gives breadth and depth to teaching and learning. Teachers were trained in the past that subjectivity in assessment is anathema, but learning how to design quality performance assessments that may include some teacher and student constructions of assessment terminology can provide valuable information on a student's progress. The trick is to bring clarity to the meaning and "look" of assessment terminology as demonstrated through student work. Students and teacher must share a common understanding of what quality "looks like."

- Changing a major teaching paradigm requires a tolerance for ambiguity. The change process is messy and uncomfortable. All of the answers to questions of curriculum, instruction, and assessment are not available up front. Teaching materials may be more fact centered than idea centered and will require an overlay of conceptual planning and instruction. The process of change is one of questioning and ongoing discovery. What is concept-process curriculum and instruction? How does it compare to what I am currently doing? Why should I change? What is the benefit for students? Where can I learn more about this method? What kinds of training will I need in the change process?

What is the principal's role in schools that elect to follow a concept-process model?

- Principals are critical to the success of any schoolwide innovation or change. Teachers look to their leaders for guidance and support. When we are talking about something as fundamental to the learning process as the structures for curriculum and instruction, then the principal must be knowledgeable. If principals bring older visions of teaching and learning to professional evaluation, they will stifle the change process.

What if class scheduling prevents students from having all of the teachers on the interdisciplinary team?

- This is a common problem—schedules, schedules, schedules! It is true. You cannot provide an integrated learning experience for students if they get only part of the package. But before schools totally restructure time into blocks and all teachers into teams, there should be 2 to 4 years of preparatory work:
  — Do teachers understand what value lies in teaming and curricular integration?
  — Do they know how and when to integrate curricula?
  — Have they learned the elements of quality teaming?
  — Are parents on board with the direction?
  — Have teachers had answers to the questions that worry them related to maintaining discipline integrity, and so on?
  — Do teachers know how time is used differently in extended instructional periods?
  — Has the planning process determined what the role of each discipline is in integrated units? Is music totally performance based in your school, for example? How will each discipline fit into the integrated teams effectively? Does a different type of music course need to be added to the curriculum, such as Music Appreciation or Music History, to have an integration tie? How about physical education? Is it totally skill based in your school? How will it tie into content-driven integration?
  — Does the administration understand and express support for teaming and integration (verbal, financial, scheduling, and planning time)?
  — How much time will be devoted to integrated curriculum and instruction during the year?

These are just some of the questions to be addressed before schools turn the dumplings upside down and stir the pot.

Why should we change our traditional curriculum and instruction models?

- President Clinton, in his 1996 inaugural campaign, stated that we need to "build a bridge to the future." And that future is very different from the 1950s. Business communities are examining and reframing their basic structures in order to be globally competitive. Education also needs to examine its basic structures. There is talk and change taking place in the organizational structures of education—we see moves toward greater site-based decision making, for example. But too often, curriculum structures still reflect narrow designs that anchor thinking in shallow waters. Performance-based education is a big step forward. But I fear that performance will fall to the level of topics and facts and will fail to draw out the conceptual understandings if curricular designs are not reframed to support deeper, complex thinking.

Summary

The heart of schooling is children and their interactions with curriculum and instruction. The heart of educational change lies with the educators who are learners themselves, and who understand that teaching and learning must change over time. We live in a complex, interactive world that calls for sophisticated abilities in accessing, using, and sharing a growing body of knowledge. Concept-process curricular models provide a clear and necessary structure for student-centered teaching strategies. A strategy by itself will not raise standards. A variety of research-based instructional strategies, framed by a concept-process structure for curriculum, can provide a strong bridge. This final chapter highlights the thoughts and works of teachers on their way to the future.

Resource A:
National Academic
Standards Order Information

The Arts

> Music Educators' Association
> 1806 Robert Fulton Avenue
> Reston, VA 20191
> 1-800-828-0229

Civics and Government

> The Center for Civic Education
> 5146 Douglas Fir Road
> Calabasas, CA 91302
> (818) 591-9321

Economics

> The National Council on Economic Education
> 1140 Avenue of the Americas
> New York, NY 10036
> (212) 730-7007

English

> International Reading Association
> 800 Barksdale Rd.
> PO Box 8139
> Newark, DE 19714
> 1-800-336-7323

Foreign Language

> ACTFL
> PO Box 1897
> Lawrence, KS 66044
> 1-800-627-0629

Geography

National Geographic Society
1145 17th St. NW
Washington, DC 20016
(202) 775-7832

Global Education

The American Forum
120 Wall Street, Suite 2600
New York, NY 10005
(212) 624-1300

History

National Center for History in the Schools
UCLA
1100 Glendon Ave, Suite 927
Box 951588
Los Angeles, CA 90095-1588
Bookstore: (310) 206-0788

Mathematics

National Council of Teachers of Mathematics
1906 Association Drive
Reston, VA 22091
(703) 620-9840

Physical Education

National Association for Sport and Physical Education
1900 Association Drive
Reston, VA 22091
1-800-321-0789

Science

National Academy Press
2101 Constitution Ave. NW
Washington, DC 20418
1-800-624-6242

Social Studies

National Council for the Social Studies
3501 Newark St. NW
Washington, DC 20016
(202) 966-7840

Resource B:
SCANS Competencies
(United States Department of Labor)

A Three-Part Foundation

Basic Skills: Reads, writes, performs arithmetic and mathematical operations, listens, and speaks

A. Reading—Locates, understands, and interprets written information in prose and in documents such as manuals, graphs, and schedules

B. Writing—Communicates thoughts, ideas, information, and messages in writing; and creates documents such as letters, directions, manuals, reports, graphs, and flow charts

C. Arithmetic and Mathematics—Performs basic computations and approaches practical problems by choosing appropriately from a variety of mathematical techniques

D. Listening—Receives, attends to, interprets, and responds to verbal messages and other cues

E. Speaking—Organizes ideas and communicates orally

Thinking Skills: Thinks creatively, makes decisions, solves problems, visualizes, knows how to learn, and reasons

A. Creative Thinking—Generates new ideas

B. Decision Making—Specifies goals and constraints, generates alternatives, considers risks, and evaluates and chooses best alternative

C. Problem Solving—Recognizes problems and devises and implements plan of action

D. Seeing Things in the Mind's Eye—Organizes and processes symbols, pictures, graphs, objects, and other information

E. Knowing How to Learn—Uses efficient learning techniques to acquire and apply new knowledge and skills

F. Reasoning—Discovers a rule or principle underlying the relationship between two or more objects and applies it when solving a problem

Personal Qualities: Displays responsibility,
self-esteem, sociability, self-management,
and integrity and honesty

A. Responsibility—Exerts a high level of effort and perseveres toward goal attainment

B. Self-Esteem—Believes in own self-worth and maintains a positive view of self

C. Sociability—Demonstrates understanding, friendliness, adaptability, empathy, and politeness in group settings

D. Self-Management—Assesses self accurately, sets personal goals, monitors progress, and exhibits self-control

E. Integrity and Honesty—Chooses ethical courses of action

Resources: Identifies, organizes,
and allocates resources

A. Time—Selects goal-relevant activities, ranks them, allocates time, and prepares and follows schedules

B. Money—Uses or prepares budgets, makes forecasts, keeps records, and makes adjustments to meet objectives

C. Material and Facilities—Acquires, stores, allocates, and uses materials or space efficiently

D. Human Resources—Assesses skills and distributes work accordingly, evaluates performance, and provides feedback

Information: Acquires and uses information

A. Acquires and Evaluates Information

B. Organizes and Maintains Information

C. Interprets and Communicates Information

D. Uses Computers to Process Information

Interpersonal: Works with others

   A. Participates as Member of a Team—Contributes to group effort
   B. Teaches Others New Skills
   C. Serves Clients or Customers—Works to satisfy customers' expectations
   D. Exercises Leadership—Communicates ideas to justify position, persuades and convinces others, responsibly challenges existing procedures and policies
   E. Negotiates—Works toward agreements involving exchange of resources, resolves divergent interests
   F. Works With Diversity—Works well with men and women of diverse backgrounds

Systems: Understands complex interrelationships

   A. Understands Systems—Knows how social, organizational, and technological systems work and operates effectively in them
   B. Monitors and Corrects Performance—Distinguishes trends, predicts impacts on system operations, diagnoses deviations in systems' performance and corrects malfunctions
   C. Improves or Designs Systems—Suggests modifications to existing systems and develops new or alternative systems to improve performance

Technology: Works with a variety of technologies

   A. Selects Technology—Chooses procedures, tools, or equipment, including computers and related technologies
   B. Applies Technology to Task—Understands overall intent and proper procedures for setup and operation of equipment
   C. Maintains and Troubleshoots Equipment—Prevents, identifies, or solves problems with equipment, including computers and other technologies

SOURCE: SCANS Competencies, U.S. Department of Labor.

Resource C:
Glossary

Concept: A mental construct that frames a set of examples sharing common attributes. One- or two-word concepts are timeless, universal, abstract, and broad. Sometimes referred to as Integrating Concepts or Focus Concepts. Concepts may be very broad macroconcepts, such as "change," "system," or "interdependence"; or they may be more topic specific, such as "organism," "habitat," or "government."

Concept-Process Integration: A curriculum design model that facilitates deeper, integrated thinking by organizing interdisciplinary content around a common topical theme, viewed through a conceptual lens.

Conceptual Theme: A topic of study that includes a concept in the title. A conceptual theme frames a conceptually based study.

Coordinated, Multidisciplinary Unit: Correlates topics, facts, and activities to a specific unit theme. Lacks a focus concept to take thinking to the integration and transfer levels.

Focus Concept: The single concept that serves as an integrating lens for a unit of study. The focus concept draws thinking above the disciplines as a common theme, issue, or problem is examined through the different subject-area perspectives. Thinking becomes "integrated" as students search for patterns and connections in the creation of new knowledge.

Generalization or Essential Understanding: Two or more *concepts* stated as a relationship—essential learnings or understandings; the "big ideas" related to the critical concepts and topics of a study. Generalizations differ from principles in that they may use qualifying terms such as *often, may,* or *can.*

Generalization Examples (Essential Understandings):

> (from courses such as mathematics, art, or design technology) *"Angles may distort the perceived dimensions of a structure."*

> (from courses such as physics, electronics technology, communications, or physical science) *"Electromagnetic waves, such as radio waves, microwaves, light waves, x-rays, and gamma rays differ only in frequency."*

> (from courses such as social studies and family and consumer sciences) *"Family and society share a reciprocal relationship."*

Guiding, Essential Questions: Specific, open-ended, thought-provoking questions that probe the factual and conceptual levels of understanding. The role of guiding questions is to create interest and a "need to know," leading toward deeper understanding of the generalizations and principles that structure the knowledge of a discipline.

Integrated, Interdisciplinary Unit: Adds a focus concept to a specific topic (topical theme) of study. Disciplines work in an interdisciplinary manner to develop understanding of the conceptual ideas that transcend the specific topic. The conceptual focus forces integrated thinking.

Integration: *Process integration* applies complex performance and skills across areas of content study. For example, reading and writing performances are used to gain and share knowledge related to a topic such as lasers. *Content integration* uses a conceptual focus to create an interdisciplinary perspective around a common theme, issue, or problem of study.

Performance Assessment: The measure of a student's progress related to what the student knows, understands, and can do. Performance assessment includes the measure of both content understanding and complex process performance.

Principle: Written in the form of a generalization, but is a truth that holds consistently through time. Principles are "laws"—such as the axioms of mathematics or the laws of science—and use no qualifying terms. Principles fall at the conceptual level of generalizations in the structure of knowledge.

Processes: Complex performances drawing on a variety of skills. Process abilities develop within the individual and grow in sophistication over time.

SCANS Competencies: A list of worker competencies and foundational skills required for successful employment published by the U.S. Department of Labor. SCANS is an acronym for Secretary's Commission on Achieving Necessary Skills.

Skills: The specific competencies required for complex process performance. Skills need to be taught directly and practiced in context. For example, some of the skills required for doing the complex performance of research include "accessing information," "identifying main ideas and details," "notetaking," and "organizing information."

Structure of Knowledge: A schema (visual or verbal) that specifies a cognitive hierarchy and relationship between facts, topics, concepts, generalizations and principles, and theories.

Topic: A category of study that implies a body of related facts to be learned. Study that is focused on topics, without a conceptual lens, results in memorization and surface understanding rather than integrated thinking and deep understanding.

Topical Theme: A topic of study that does not include a concept in the title. A topical theme frames a fact-based study.

References

Bailey, T., & Merritt, D. (1995). *Making sense of industry-based skill standards* (Booklet). Berkeley: University of California Press, National Center for Research in Vocational Education.

Beane, J. (Ed.). (1995). *Toward a coherent curriculum.* Alexandria, VA: Association for Supervision and Curriculum Development.

Caine, R. N., & Caine, G. (1991). *Teaching and the human brain.* Alexandria, VA: Association for Supervision and Curriculum Development.

Caine, R. N., & Caine, G. (1997). *Education on the edge of possibility.* Alexandria, VA: Association for Supervision and Curriculum Development.

Center for Civic Education. (1994). *National standards for civics and government.* Calabasas, CA: Author.

Geography Education Standards Project. (1994). *Geography for life: The national geography standards.* Washington, DC: National Geographic Society.

Hayes-Jacobs, H. (1997). *Mapping the big picture: Integrating curriculum and assessment, K-12.* Alexandria, VA: Association for Supervision and Curriculum Development.

National Center for History in the Schools. (1996). *National standards for history.* Los Angeles: Author.

National Council of Social Studies (NCSS). (1994). *National standards for the social studies.* Washington, DC: Author.

National Council of Teachers of Mathematics. (1989). *Curriculum and evaluation standards for school mathematics.* Reston, VA: Author.

National Council on Economic Education. (1997). *National content standards in economics.* New York: Author.

National Research Council. (1996). *National science education standards.* Washington, DC: National Academy Press.

Perkins, D. (1992). *Smart schools: Better thinking and learning for every child.* New York: Free Press.

Rogers, S., & Graham, S. (1997). *The high performance toolbox.* Evergreen, CO: Peak Learning Systems.

Secretary's Commission on Achieving Necessary Skills (SCANS). (1991). *What work requires of schools: A SCANS report for America 2000.* Washington, DC: U.S. Department of Labor, Secretary's Commission on Achieving Necessary Skills.

Taba, H. (1966). *Teaching strategies and cognitive functioning in elementary school children* (Cooperative research project). Washington, DC: Office of Education, U.S. Department of Health, Education, and Welfare.

Viadero, D. (1997, April 2). Surprise! Analyses link curriculum, TIMSS scores. *Education Week,* p. 6.

Index

**CORWIN
PRESS**

The Corwin Press logo—a raven striding across an open book—represents the happy union of courage and learning. We are a professional-level publisher of books and journals for K-12 educators, and we are committed to creating and providing resources that embody these qualities. Corwin's motto is "Success for All Learners."